124347
£42.50

THE DEPTH OF SHALLOW CULTURE

Studies in Comparative Social Science
∾ A series edited by Stephen K. Sanderson ∾

Titles Available

Revolutions: A Worldwide Introduction to Political and Social Change,
Stephen K. Sanderson (2005)

Plunging to Leviathan: Exploring the World's Political Future,
Robert Bates Graber (2005)

The Depth of Shallow Culture: The High Art
of Shoes, Movies, Novels, Monsters, and Toys
Albert J. Bergesen (2006)

Studying Societies and Cultures: Marvin Harris's
Cultural Materialism and Its Legacy
Edited by Lawrence A. Kuznar and Stephen K. Sanderson (2006)

THE DEPTH OF SHALLOW CULTURE
THE HIGH ART OF SHOES, MOVIES, NOVELS, MONSTERS, AND TOYS

Albert J. Bergesen

Paradigm Publishers

Boulder • London

Copyright © 2006 by Paradigm Publishers

Published in the United States by Paradigm Publishers, 3360 Mitchell Lane Suite E, Boulder, Colorado 80301 USA.

Paradigm Publishers is the trade name of Birkenkamp & Company, LLC, Dean Birkenkamp, President and Publisher.

Library of Congress Cataloging-in-Publication

Bergesen, Albert.
   The depth of shallow culture : the high art of shoes, movies, novels, monsters, and toys / Albert J. Bergesen.
      p. cm.
   Includes bibliographical references and index.
   Contents: Introduction : the depth of shallow culture—The baroque sneaker : how the history of the tennis shoe recapitulates Giorgio Vasari's Life cycle of art styles—Rambo and Don Quixote : cultural icons of national decline—A sociology of monsters : making mythical creatures in the United States and Japan—A sociology of toys : how Transformers and Spiderman embody the philosophies of East and West—Bringing the art object back in : toward a new realism in the sociology of culture.
   ISBN-13: 978-1-59451-273-5 (hc)
   ISBN-10: 1-59451-273-6 (hc)
   1. Popular culture.   2. Material culture.   3. Civilization, Modern–21st century.
I. Title.
   CB430.B47 2006
   306.0973—dc22

   BER

                                                                    2006012365

Designed and Typeset in New Baskerville by Straight Creek Bookmakers.

10 09 08 07 06 1 2 3 4 5

Contents

Acknowledgments

Four people were directly involved in turning these chapters into a book. Steve Sanderson originally asked me to write a book on a specific topic for his book series. I responded with an alternative book proposal, and after much discussion via e-mail, this book took shape in its present form. Steve also made a number of valuable editorial suggestions and did the initial copyediting of each chapter. Mitch Allen more than encouraged me when things looked dark. I won't forget his support when I needed it. Dean Birkenkamp listened to me, read some chapters, and then agreed to publish the book. For that I am very grateful. Susie Bergesen, my wife, combined all of the above: listened, gave comments, provided support, and pushed me to make the project the best I could. Thanks, all of you.

Albert J. Bergesen

CHAPTER ONE

Introduction

The Depth of Shallow Culture

POPULAR CULTURE, ALMOST BY DEFINITION, is shallow. Designed for a very wide swath of the population, it must stay at a low level of sophistication to appeal to as many consumers as possible. If you cannot assume your audience has advanced schooling, or knowledge about, say, the opera, the symphony, playwrights, or drama, then you cannot engage in references to esoteric subjects or complex philosophical ideas. Modern popular culture is designed for the broad public with a commercial interest in mind; the desire is to entertain, not to educate or stimulate. It is not designed to embody or express deep philosophy or be similar in stylistic form to the fine arts. We speak of Baroque painting, but not in any serious way of Baroque footwear, except in a loose metaphorical sense about a busy and messy shoe. The history of European painting comprised of Baroque, Mannerist, or Rococo styling is not, by and large, applied to the history of footwear. Nor would reasonable scholarship attend to similarities between, say, one of the world's great novels, *Don Quixote*, and the Rambo films starring Sylvester Stallone. Children's toys are understood to perform socialization functions, but not particularly to embody some of the finer points of complex philosophy and religious dogma. Nor are cultural objects all of the same aesthetic value, either. Baroque paintings are different from Baroque sneakers; Rambo films are B-movies whereas

1

Cervantes's novel is a great work of art; and toys are toys, and certainly philosophy is philosophy. As Kipling might have said: Art is art and popular culture is popular culture.

But if we can put aesthetic value aside for the moment, there does seem to be enough stylistic and thematic commonality across art and popular culture to warrant a comparative analysis between high and low culture. Distinctions between great art and ordinary or poor art, or between mass culture and elite culture, do not preclude objects from being studied and theorized. Thus, to identify principles of Baroque style in a basketball sneaker and a Rubens painting is to equate them as embodying a common architecture of form, but it is not to say that they are necessarily equal aesthetically. From this point of view, it is the purpose of this book to bring to the reader's attention the sophistication of stylistic form and philosophical depth of thematic content that often characterizes works of shallow popular culture. To do this I will make comparisons of different instances of one kind of popular culture (sneakers, the subject of Chapter 2); different kinds of culture (novels and movies, the subject of Chapter 3); different cultural principles that produce different kinds of mythical creatures in different civilizational contexts (King Kong and Godzilla, the focus of Chapter 4); and finally, different kinds of toys embodying different philosophical outlooks (such as Transformers and the idea of reincarnation, which are discussed in Chapter 5).

Theoretical Perspectives

The Exogenous Model

Such is the content of the book. What of its theoretical focus? Here I will draw on three theoretical perspectives within the sociology of culture. The first perspective is best represented in arguments put forth by the classic sociology of Karl Marx and Emile Durkheim, who argue that culture—popular, high, or otherwise—is shaped and influenced, or actually mirrors and reflects, the power configuration of the society within which it is produced. The key assumption is that those causal factors that are employed to explain cultural objects lie essentially outside the object itself, hence the Exogenous Model.

Which of society's various groupings—classes, organizations, status groups, and so forth—is chosen as the explanation varies with the theorist in question. Obviously, for Karl Marx the key element was the economic class position of the author. In a more comparative vein, he focused on the economy as a total mode of production, so that under, say, the feudal mode of production one would expect certain kinds of culture to be produced that would be different from what would be produced under capitalism. Here the causal variable of a mode of production constituted the bedrock, foundation, or base upon which arose any number of cultural activities, from laws and social attitudes to novels, plays, movies, video games, or toys. Because such cultural activities, elite or popular, are dependent upon such a base, they came to be called the superstructure, and the overall model the Base-Superstructure Model.

Emile Durkheim (1965 [1912]) employed a type of Base-Super-structure Model. However, his base did not consist of economic classes but rather the collective sense of solidarity of the entire society. For Durkheim, a "collective representation" meant a piece of culture that represented, or stood for, the collective reality of the group as a corporate whole. It could be said that Durkheim formulated a more politically neutral Base-Superstructure Model, for the collective representation was not explicitly identified as being in the service of the material interests of any particular group. Marxian and Durkheimian theory are often contrasted, but this need not be so, for what is Marxian class consciousness but Durkheimian collective representations for a particular economic class that have been internalized by its occupants?

For such exogenous models to work, one needs to identify some aspect of society that can plausibly be linked to some aspect of culture. In Chapter 3 the independent variable is national decline—societies losing their dominant position within a larger international network of societies—and the dependent variable consists of common cultural themes within Cervantes's novel and the Rambo movies. The theoretical argument is that objective conditions of national decline generate collective anxiety and angst that manifest themselves in the mythical figures of Don Quixote and Rambo. The gap between what they believe to be the case and what actually is the case is a metaphor for the growing gap between past hegemonic prominence and the new reality of national decline.

The Endogenous Model

In what could be called an Endogenous Model the focus shifts to the internal subjective meanings held within culture itself. Of the three great founding sociologists, Max Weber, with his focus on the meaning of social action as one of its determinants, is probably most closely associated with this outlook. Weber's famous argument about the Protestant ethic and the spirit of capitalism is perhaps the best-known example of endogenous cultural processes. For Weber, the world's religions have their own internal meaning expressed in their dogma and ethics. Individuals' understanding (*verstehen*) of what they mean provides the basis for their behavior. This Weberian emphasis upon the pure understanding of cultural ideas was the first reaction against the Marx/Durkheim Base-Superstructure Model. From Weber's writings in the early twentieth century through the neo-Weberian authors of today, there has been a persistent tradition of analyzing culture as an autonomous realm.

There is another more recent reaction to the Exogenous Model by sociologists who have felt that the argument for a simple reflection theory of culture was inadequate (DiMaggio 1977; Swidler 1986; Wuthnow 1987; DeNora 1991; Sewell 1992; Fine 1992; Bielby and Bielby 1999; Lieberson 2003; Kaufman 2004; Peterson and Anand 2004). They argue that there are numerous examples where it is hard to find a specific class interest, corporate business interest, or political power interest that is being directly served by attributes of an element of popular or elite culture. The gap or distance between society's collective interest, or even an economic class interest, and a cultural form seemed too large. Therefore, something needed to be inserted between the broad sense of society and the specifics of a cultural object, like the production process in which a piece of art or popular culture was manufactured. Within the sociology of culture this is known as the "production of culture" perspective (Peterson and Anand 2004). As a halfway position, culture's cause is still somewhat exogenous—the production process (making a movie, selling a novel, market pressures, and so on)—but it moves us now closer to the cultural object itself. It isn't some distant capitalist class that is somehow getting its way with the content of a novel by mechanisms that cannot be understood, but rather the specific business practices of the publishing industry, or of advertising firms, or of market demand.

That is, something closer to the cultural object itself is theorized to be affecting the shape and content of the object.

But there is still one more step to be taken, and that is to conceive of a full endogeneity, or complete autonomy, of the cultural process. In this view, culture operates according to its own cultural laws, not Durkheimian principles of group solidarity, Marxian ideas about class position, or intermediary mechanisms like the market, cultural gatekeepers, or some aspect of the production process. This fully endogenous approach involves looking for processes within cultural objects themselves (for a recent review see Kaufman 2004). The question here is whether there is an internal logic to culture above and beyond the logic of the society in which the culture is nested or the logic of the production process that makes culture's material form possible. One of the best-known examples is Lieberson's (2003) study of shifts in children's names, where there is a slow discernible change that does not seem to correspond to changes within the larger society. Chapter 2 provides an example of what seems to be a purely endogenous cultural process, the evolution of style patterns in the history of the sneaker. Such a perspective might also be used to understand the philosophical assumptions embedded in ordinary children's toys (Chapter 5), or the civilizational algorithms by which Eastern and Western societies produce a wide range of popular cultural objects (Chapter 4).

Overview of the Chapters

Chapter 2 will ask whether the life cycle of art historical styles identified by the Renaissance art historian Vasari also characterizes the history of the modern tennis shoe, or sneaker. That is, do high culture and popular culture follow similar principles of stylistic development that have heretofore gone unnoticed? I suggest the answer is yes, for the status of the cultural object as "high" or "low" is irrelevant to whether its stylistic history exhibits an identifiable pattern. We know that from the High Renaissance to Mannerism and the Baroque, and then on to Neoclassicism and the Rococo, there are identifiable changes in line, plane, symmetry, and other dimensions of the formal composition of Western art (Wolfflin 1950). Chapter 2 asks: Do the principles of these art historical styles also characterize the history of the modern sneaker; that is, does the sneaker follow the same stages identified by Vasari for classic Greek sculpture and Renaissance painting?

Chapter 3 considers another instance of often unseen depth to popular culture by exploring thematic commonality in two works considered embodiments of high and low cultural expression: Cervantes's great novel *Don Quixote* and the very shallow Rambo movies starring Sylvester Stallone. The chapter asks: Could Rambo be Don Quixote? Not literally, of course, but could they both epitomize a common theme that reflected the common international position of sixteenth-century Spain and the late-twentieth-century United States? The art historian Arnold Hauser (1959:145) argued that the "tragedy of the individual knight [Don Quixote] is repeated on a wider scale in the fate of the chivalrous nation par excellence [Spain]," and this chapter wonders if a similar relationship exists between the individual Special Forces soldier (John Rambo) and the anticommunist nation par excellence (the United States). The sociological basis for this comparison lies in the fact that there is a great deal of similarity between these countries inasmuch as both were entering periods of imperial or hegemonic decline after having earlier been the predominant global economic powers of their time. Both produced narratives (novel and film) that had a large international following and dealt with virtually the same theme: dramatizing the gap between a national ethos (Spanish chivalry and a U.S. Special Forces Green Beret ethos) and objective historical conditions. Don Quixote took a medieval Spanish worldview and applied it where it was no longer applicable; the result was a disaster. John Rambo took a Vietnam War ethic of guerrilla fighting and applied it to Oregon; the result was a similar disaster. Both characters were delusional, both were caricatures of chivalric ideals, and both generated humor as audiences in many countries read about and watched their adventures and foolish strivings in a world to which they no longer belonged.

Chapter 4 suggests that if the next hegemonic center of world production is East Asia, then for the first time the transition from one leading economic zone (North America) to another (East Asia) will also involve the rise of a center of global culture within a non-Western civilization. Studies of the rise of Japan and China in the world economy should be supplemented by analyses of distinctly Asian mythological themes in global popular culture. This task is begun here with a comparison of monster-making cultural practices in both

East and West. In the West, mythical monsters seem constructed by a logic that mixes properties of natural creatures, such as goat + man = satyr, or supernatural power + woman = Wonder Woman. But in the East, we see less mixing and more creating of entirely new mythical beings. These beings are very often distinctly supernatural, such as the ancient image of the dragon, or such contemporary creatures as Godzilla, Transformers, and Pokemon (pocket monsters). Chapter 4 identifies two different civilizational logics, or sets of cultural rules, for making mythical creatures. One can be called the Mixing Model, which seems to be activated more often in the cultural construction of Western imaginary beings (whether in classic myths or in popular culture). The second I call the Essentially Other Model, which seems more prevalent in Eastern cultures. The origin of these differences remains something of an open question, but a working hypothesis linking different cultural algorithms with different distributions of power within political systems is proposed.

Chapter 5 raises the question of whether there is an association between the shape, look, and operation of children's toys and a society's background philosophy. In short, can shallow toys embody deeper religious and philosophical systems of thought? Can Transformer toys, built so that their body parts move and allow them to "transform" from one state of being to another (from, say, a truck to a person), be the embodiment of the philosophy of reincarnation? Alternatively, Western toys, which also have flexible parts, can only be manipulated in ways that realize different behaviors within a single material incarnation. The action figure GI Joe, for instance, is built to move his arms, legs, and head, but only in order to perform human or soldier behaviors. He can throw a grenade, shoot a rifle, run, and jump, but no matter how much a child twists and turns a GI Joe action figure, he cannot be transformed into a truck, car, boat, airplane, or beast. A child could, though, do that with a Transformer toy.

Chapter 6 concludes the book with a discussion of some assumptions in the sociology of art and popular culture. Specifically, I challenge the idea that cultural objects gain their meaning through the interpretations they are given. Artworks and popular culture are not neutral material objects whose meaning can only arise from added human interpretation upon reading, viewing, hearing, or being played with. That is an old assumption rooted in German idealist philosophy and early-twentieth-century Saussurian theory about the arbitrary nature of the sign (the art object) and the thing it signifies (the meaning of the art). The sociology of art today is built on these two assumptions, which has created a de facto neutered art object awaiting an infusion of meaning from the surrounding art world, cultural classificatory grids, worldviews, class-based viewing habits, and so forth.

But nothing could be further from the truth. The art object is no more incapable of emitting meaning than a sentence. Art forms, analogous to linguistic grammar, participate in determining the meaning that composition will elicit. Chapter 6 argues for a new sociology of art that brings the art object back into the heart of the sociology of culture. There is nothing wrong with the study of museums, critics, art world opinions, and all the other social institutions that generate opinions about works of art. But what must be realized is that these are secondary opinions as best—that the artwork, within its very syntactic form, has already made a statement, and that meaning enters art prior to interpretation.

CHAPTER TWO

The Baroque Sneaker

How the History of the Tennis Shoe Recapitulates
Giorgio Vasari's Life Cycle of Art Styles

LINKING SNEAKERS WITH STYLES IN ART is not a new idea. It is usually associated with artists decorating traditional sneakers, thereby making them "art objects." My interest here, though, is more in line with traditional art history and its sequence of major style categories, such as the progression from the High Renaissance through Mannerist to the Baroque and the Rococo. Just as Gramsci spoke of organic intellectuals naturally arising within a society, so we can think of something like organic cultural styles, sequences of shapes and forms that seem to arise naturally within the ebb and flow of normal social and economic life.

The study of style in this sense is usually limited to the fine arts, where applying the term Baroque to a building or painting is common. But what of ordinary footwear like the sneaker? Could the terms Baroque or Rococo be used to characterize sneaker style, and, more interestingly, is it possible that something like the life cycle of art styles identified by the great Renaissance Italian art historian Giorgio Vasari in the sixteenth century is at work in the history of sneaker styles? I suggest the answer is yes, and that from marble and paint to rubber and canvas are materials that can be structured in distinctive ways that reflect underlying principles of style.

9

More specifically, the idea that styles of art go through a life cycle—from an awkward adolescence to an idealized maturity, and then decline in old age into a more twisted and convoluted form—can be traced to the writings of Vasari (1977). Such a pattern can be seen in the progression of ancient Greek sculpture from the simple, awkward, stiff, and roughly hewn (Archaic period), through the more balanced, symmetrical, and elegant (Classic period), to the more emotional and convulsive (Hellenistic period). The Archaic appeared with the emergence of full-sized statuary in the seventh century BCE, epitomized by the carved figures of male *kouros* (youths) and female *kore* (maidens). These were produced in large numbers and their general outline remained remarkably stable over the period. The Classic style followed during the fifth century BCE when figures were more animated. They were posed in balanced, proportional, symmetrical ways, with a somewhat unemotional eternal expression. Well-known examples include the *Discobolus* (Discus Thrower) (c. 450 BCE), the spear-bearer by Polykleitos (c. 440 BCE), and the frieze of the Parthenon. A Classic style arises from the balanced assemblage of components, which retain their own discrete integrity while at the same time being part of a larger artistic whole. The Classic period was then followed by Hellenistic styling of the third century BCE, in which the harmony and detached nature of the Classic was replaced by more uncontrolled bodily responses, along with more expressiveness and a greater commitment to reality in the representation of figures. Well-known examples include the *Dying Gaul* (c. 230–220 BCE), the *Nike of Samothrace* (c. 200–190 BCE), and *The Lacoon Group,* (first century CE), which showed the death of Lacoon and his two sons. Vasari noted this pattern and went on to identify a similar style cycle in the European painting of his day: Early Renaissance, High Renaissance, and Late Renaissance/Early Baroque. Today we would elaborate that scheme and place a style called Mannerism right after the Renaissance but before the Baroque, and place the Rococo right after the Baroque.

To these fine art examples from Greek sculpture and European painting I would add another instance of a life cycle of expression: the patterned configuration of color, shape, and stitching of the ordinary sneaker. The history of the modern sneaker reveals stylistic principles along the lines of the sculpture and painting of the past; one can identify something like a life cycle of sneaker styles, or an art history of the sneaker, that progresses through a very similar set of style phases. We can identify an *Archaic* sneaker, followed in time by a *Classic,* a *Mannerist,* a *Baroque,* and finally a *Rococo* sneaker. The most general sociology of culture point here is that principles for configuring raw material into recognizable stylistic forms are not limited to the fine arts. Such patterns can be found in ordinary footwear as well. Cultural styling is, in this sense, irrepressible. It transcends evaluative distinctions of highbrow or lowbrow, fine art or mass art, elite or popular culture. The social act of styling can be employed to structure stone, yielding the discus-thrower by Myron (c. 450 BCE), or to arrange paint on canvas, yielding Leonardo Da Vinci's *The Last Supper* (1495–1498), or to combine leather and synthetic materials creating Nike's *Air Jordan I* sneaker in the 1980s. Regardless of national culture or historical period, there are identifiable patterns to cultural objects. Before turning to the specifics of this style cycle, we need to consider a brief history of the emergence of the modern sneaker.

Sneaker History

Forerunners of what is variously called the athletic shoe, jogging shoe, basketball shoe, tennis shoe, or just plain sneaker can be found in Great Britain, Germany, and the United States. Going back to the middle of the nineteenth century, a forerunner of such a canvas-topped shoe appeared in Britain in the 1860s when it became popular to go to the beach. The shoe was called the "Plimsoll" after Samuel Plimsoll, who worked to have a white line drawn on the side of merchant ships to show cargo weight. Plimsolls were worn in the first modern Olympics in Athens in 1896.

In Germany the origin of the sneaker-type shoe was associated with performance sports (Strasser and Becklund 1993). The Dassler family made competitive gymnastics and soccer shoes after World War I, and these shoes appeared in the Amsterdam Olympics of 1928. Jesse Owens won four gold medals wearing Dassler track shoes in the 1936 Berlin Olympics. The Dasslers were innovators in the design of competitive athletic shoes, bringing out the first shoes for ice and the first track shoe with replaceable spikes. After World War II the Dassler brothers Adi and Rudi had a falling out, with each starting his own shoe company. Adi Dassler called his company "Addas," which evolved into "Adidas"—a combination of his nickname Adi and the family name Dassler. Brother Rudi named his company "Puma." The new Adidas company kept the two support strips from earlier Dassler athletic shoes wrapped over the ball of the foot and added a third strip, thereby creating the well-known Adidas logo of three stripes on the side of the shoe. Adidas and Puma dominated the world market in high-performance athletic sneakers into the 1970s.

In the United States sneakers became popular when the U.S. Rubber Company invented a process called "vulcanization," which attached rubber to canvas. The company went on to produce a shoe with a rubber sole and canvas upper called the "sneaker" because it didn't make the squeaking sound of leather shoes. These shoes were first named "Peds," in honor of the feet, but trademark problems led to the name "Veds," which didn't seem exciting enough, and so a new name arose mixing "kids," who were the target market, and "peds" to produce the name "Keds." These sneakers were first marketed in 1916, and by the middle of the twentieth century millions of pairs were being sold.

The ancestor of today's basketball sneaker was the 1912 Spaulding high-top that had uppers of black kangaroo leather and a gum rubber "suction sole" (Resnick 1988). At about the same time, a New England manufacturer named Marquis M. Converse started the Converse Rubber Company. In 1917 Converse introduced a canvas rubber-soled basketball shoe, which in 1923 was renamed the "Chuck Taylor All-Star" shoe in honor of Chuck Taylor, a barnstorming former basketball player who demonstrated and sold the sneaker for Converse. By the 1920s the Converse All-Star sneaker was the most popular basketball shoe, dominating the market until the rise of Adidas's "Pro Model" in the 1960s and Puma's low-top suede shoe in the 1970s. Also in the early 1970s a University of Oregon track man, Phil Knight, and his coach, Bill Bowerman, combined to produce sneakers for jogging and track, forming a company (Blue Ribbon Sports) that would later be renamed Nike. Like the Dasslers, they were also innovators, introducing a foam wedge under the heel that allowed easier jogging on streets, a nylon upper that lightened running shoes, and in 1979 an air bubble under the heel for further comfort. Perhaps the most legendary of experimentations with improving athletic shoes was Bowerman's design for a new type of sole for running shoes. He poured latex rubber into a waffle iron, which he then cut to the outline of a foot and attached to a sneaker. The "waffle"-sole running shoe was one of Nike's best-known early trademarks.

Life Cycle of Sneaker Styles

In going through the sneaker style cycle, I will rely upon distinctions made by the art historian Heinrich Wolfflin (1950, 1952, 1966) in his discussion of abstract principles of style.[1] He thought these principles were general enough to be seen in painting, sculpture, drawing, and architecture. To this list I would like to add sneakers. We begin with what I will call the Archaic Sneaker.

The Archaic Sneaker

> It is the peculiar nature of art always to be crude, stiff, and unreal in the beginning.
>
> —*Giorgio Vasari*

The first versions of the modern sneaker were introduced in the early twentieth century. In 1912 Spaulding brought out a basketball shoe, in 1916 Keds were introduced, and in 1917 Converse inaugurated what would become the Chuck Taylor All-Star Shoe (see Figure 2.1). Until the 1970s the design of such sneakers was dominated by a simple and rudimentary style composed of a thick rubber sole attached to a coarse canvas upper with stainless-steel eyelets for broad, flat cotton laces. Colors were, by and large, limited. The shoes were most often white, but the Converse basketball shoe was famously black, and Sperry's "Top Sider" deck shoe was navy blue. Function might dictate variation in shoe elements, but not in basic design. Given the rugged wear and tear of competitive basketball, the Converse All-Star shoe had high tops so that laces could be drawn tight around the ankle for added support, and a sturdier tire-tread sole to grip the floor. For more casual wear, Keds had lighter soles and low tops, and the Sperry Top Sider had zig-zag cuts on the bottom to prevent slipping on the wet decks of sailboats. But underneath all these differences the style was basically the same: coarse canvas upper in a limited number of colors attached to a relatively thick white rubber sole. It was the hallmark of the Archaic sneaker style, and it would last until the 1970s.

Figure 2.1. The Archaic Sneaker's coarse, roughly hewn material and thick rubber sole (Photokaya)

To more clearly explicate the principles of this style I turn to the Converse All-Star shoe, which dominated basketball courts from the 1920s through the 1960s. As seen in Figure 2.1, this early sneaker looks and feels chunky and crude, made as it is of raw materials barely shaped or modulated above the most basic functions: sole to grip the surface, upper to enclose the foot, and laces to draw it tight. The outer sole is a wide band of white rubber, extending, with little indentation, in a straight line from toe to heel. This heavy, thick sole gave the shoe a very solid and grounded feel. All that were accented or articulated were the most rudimentary elements of the shoe: rubber sole, canvas upper, cotton laces. In this regard, the early sneaker shares a similar Archaic feel to early Greek sculpture epitomized by the carved figures of male *kouros* and female *kore*. If the Converse conveyed a minimal sense of shoeness, the *kouros* conveyed a minimal sense of the human body. They were crudely carved, with little naturalness other than articulating basic body parts: broad shoulders, arms that hung to the side, largely undifferentiated torso, and one leg slightly forward of the other.

The Classic Sneaker

As Archaic Greek sculpture gave way to the balance and proportion of the Classic style, so did the Archaic sneaker give way in the 1970s to a new more elegantly styled shoe. Converse All-Stars, Keds, Sperry Top Siders, and other early Archaic sneakers continued to be manufactured in their original style, but by the 1970s noticeable changes in sneaker styling began to appear. The growing popularity of jogging and aerobics coincided with the introduction of newly styled shoes from major manufacturers (Adidas, Nike, Reebok, Converse), and principles of style that had held sway since the early twentieth century began to give way to a new look in sneaker design. A renewed interest in professional basketball and signature shoes named after star players made the basketball sneaker rise in popularity and stylistic leadership during the 1970s. The rise of the new shoes accompanied the decline in popularity of the long-established Converse All-Star basketball sneaker, in favor of Adidas's leather-topped "Pro Model," Puma's suede shoe, and an emerging line of Nike basketball sneakers, with the most famous being the "Air Jordan" introduced in the mid-1980s.

What is characteristic of these new Classic sneakers is their departure from the rudimentary simplicity of the earlier Archaic style. With the Archaic sneaker there was something of an afterglow of raw material as styling effects were deeply submerged in canvas and rubber. But all this changed when form and line were no longer imprisoned in rubber and canvas, but now through color and embroidery come to articulate a shoe's constituent elements of heel, toe, upper, and sole. Once these forms had been freed from the bulkiness of their underlying raw material, they could be combined in a new compositional totality under the instructions of Classic principles of proportion, balance, symmetry, and clarity. With this change we witness the rise of the Classic stage of sneaker design.

The early Classic sneaker was often monochromatic, with only the emblem of the manufacturer placed on the inner and outer side of the shoe. For Nike it was the "swoosh," (✔), for Adidas the three strips (/ / /) (see Figure 2.2), and with Converse sometimes a star (★) and other times a star with a "❮" in front (❮★). Going into the 1980s, more style elements were added, as colored accent strips were placed around the heel, ankle, and toe, and colored embroidered stitching was used to articulate the basic contour of the sneaker. This period of the 1970s and 1980s was the period of High Classicism in sneaker styles. (For an example of such simple elegance, see Figure 2.2.)

The sneaker that most clearly epitomized the new High Classic style was Nike's first signature shoe, the "Air Jordan I" (for a facsimile of that shoe, see Figure 2.3). The shoe was named after Michael Jordan, a promising University of North Carolina basketball player who left college after his junior year to play for the Chicago Bulls of the National Basketball Association. Until then most signature shoes were from Adidas and Converse, but an aggressive new shoe company, Nike, made the decision to create a signature shoe and name it after Jordan because of his extraordinary athletic ability and promise as a professional athlete. The sneaker, and Jordan, were an immediate success. When Jordan wore his new red-and-black shoes in the mid-1980s, one sportswriter wrote, "Michael Jordan is not the most incredible, the most colorful, the most amazing, the most flashy, or the most mind-boggling thing in the NBA. His shoes are" (quoted in Strasser and Becklund 1993:451). This sneaker turned out to be the most successful athletic endorsement ever, selling more than $100

Figure 2.2. The Classic Sneaker's clear simple line and proportional balance between accent marks (Photokaya)

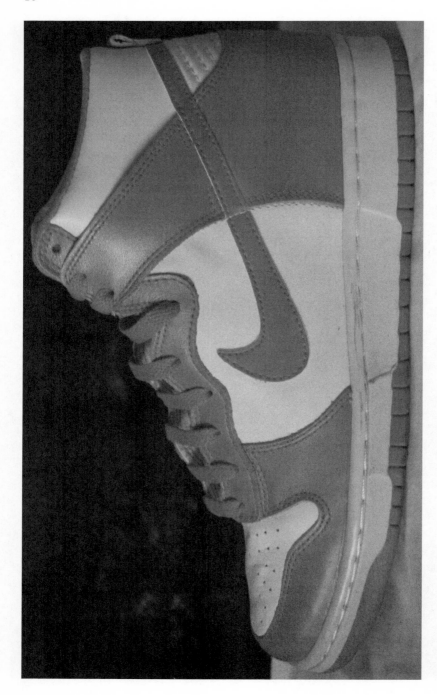

Figure 2.3 A facsimile of the Air Jordan I (Photokaya)

million worth of shoes in one year. Nike was not the leading shoe company at the time, but due in no small measure to the popularity of the Air Jordan line, it soon came to dominate the worldwide sneaker market. In 1984 Nike had a net income of about $40 million, and by the end of 1998 that figure had increased to about $800 million (Halberstam 1999:413).

In the battle between the principles of style that frame, and the raw material that is framed, raw material won out in the case of the Archaic sneaker. Framing principles of style were simply overcome by coarse monocolored canvas and a heavy rubber sole, giving the early sneaker its simple and rudimentary feel.

In the case of the *kouros* statuary, it was constrained by its vertical framing, where the body was straight up, head centered, arms and legs straight down, and eyes forward. The arms are close to the body, and so the whole effect is of a single piece with slight articulation of the body parts. The same general principles characterize the Archaic Converse sneaker. If stood on end the effect is similar to that of the *kouros*. The sole is straight from heel to toe, and there is minimal articulation of heel, toe, and laces. The *Discobolus* is a similar male figure, but it is shaped by the principles of the Classic style. Now the torso twists, the arms are apart from the body, and the knees are bent; the left foot touches only on the toe while the right lands on full footing; the arm is raised, holding the discuss with thumb spread away from fingers; and the body musculature is clearer in definition. Here the movement of the body constitutes a contour and line that leads the eye, as happens with the Classic Air Jordan shoe, where the red markings lead the eye around the shoe, articulating the different components and their sense of proportional balance. The dominance of material over form began to shift in the other direction in the 1970s, as seen in Figures 2.2 and 2.3. In the case of the Air Jordan I, the shoe possessed a Classic sense of balance and proportion in both its color and its form. Colorwise it was composed of roughly equal portions of red, white, and black, which did not bleed over the borders of the embroidered pieces of shoe material, as color was constrained within form. In that first Air Jordan shoe, white was a flat background and red served as a clear unbroken line that constitutes the shoe's main expressive effect, as it ran from the top of the upper down over the lacing eyelets to the ball of the foot, and then in a wide graceful circle around the outer edge of the toe as a band of red embroidery. It gave the shoe a clear outline and provided the eye an easy line to follow as the shoe's contour is expressed through the red outline, making the sluggishness of the earlier Converse All-Star disappear. In earlier Archaic sneakers the thick rubber sole seemed to hold the shoe to the ground. With the new Classic sneaker, the Air Jordan's white band on the side of its outer sole, sandwiched between the red of the bottom and the red of the heel and toe, made the sneaker seem to float on air.

Because of the constant coloration of uppers, earlier Archaic sneakers could not articulate the presence of heel, toe, or laces in any pronounced fashion. The new styling of the Jordan, with color around the back of the heel and striping to outline the toe and shoelace eyelets, allowed each component to receive a relative equality of emphasis. This was clearly a hallmark of the classic style that Wolfflin himself would have recognized. While some forms were bigger than others, none was big enough to constitute the sneaker's main effect and thereby dwarf the independent effect of the other colors, stitchings, or accentuated parts of the shoe (heel, toe, sole). The black "swosh" logo on the shoe's side was also proportional to the other areas of color and form, such that in this sneaker no one element dominated any other, realizing the effect of separate elements, each with its own independent integrity, yet brought into a balanced and symmetrical overall design. This was Wolfflin's point that in Classic styling small effects are small enough not to disturb large ones, yet not so small that they lose their integrity as individual forms. Raw material, the dominant effect of the earlier Archaic sneaker, now gave way to the experience of balanced composition. The block-like presence of the Archaic sneaker's coarse canvas and solid rubber receded in the face of the interrelationship of the shoe's subcomponents that defined the Classic sneaker.

The Mannerist Sneaker

By the later 1980s shoe styles were again changing, as noted in a description taken from a popular magazine.

> The late 1980s ... ushered in an era of increasingly complex (and hideous) shoe design.... Anti-inversion straps. Velcro. Neon highlights. Neon-high-lighted anti-inversion straps that velcroed over vents. It was hard to believe the basketball shoe—which started as an eyeleted piece of canvas fused to a simple rubber sole—had become so complicated.

But by the early 90s, the feet of NBA players had become more and more weighted down by technological "advances." Zippers. Gel.... Velcro pockets.... By the early 90s, even the Air Jordan was weighted down with straps, embroidery and a latch-hook patch. Luckily, designers came back to their senses ... [ending] the nightmare the players of the late 80s and early 90s endured. (*Slam Presents Kicks* 1999:13, 14)

Some of the above style issues can be seen in the example of the Mannerist Sneaker shown in Figure 2.4. To appreciate the difference between the earlier Classic and the emerging Mannerist style, bring your eye to the sole of the shoe in Figure 2.4 and note that the continuous smooth and clear sole line of the Classic sneaker is now gone. In its place is a line that waves and is broken up in different colors and materials, yielding a somewhat jumbled and discontinuous effect. Look next at the upper and see plastic straps from heel to top laces and then again in the front of the shoe. In between lies mesh material stitched in with no apparent reason other than a somewhat randomly placed decorative effect.

In art history the period between the High Renaissance and the full Baroque had some distinctive stylistic characteristics that were at first designated Late Renaissance or Early Baroque but over time came to be called Mannerist. This in-between period was characterized by crowded, jumbled, agitated, and distorted composition, and in the history of the sneaker there is a similar period between the High Classicism of the mid-1980s and the Baroque styling of the 1990s. In the new style, classic forms lost much of their proportion and balanced order but were not as yet fused into the continuous composite whole that would be the forthcoming Baroque sneaker style. Losing a sense of order that structures forms, yet not dominated by a single form, sneaker composition became crowded and jumbled. This style, though, is transitional, reflecting a struggle between the Classic organizing principles of the past that linked disparate elements into a structured compositional totality and the coming Baroque principles of a singular colossal mass of fused forms.

This struggle between form and mass gave the Mannerist style its highly agitated appearance.[2] The process is one of cultural lag. In effect, the Classic compositional forces of the past try to hold the shoe's subforms in their place, as they are struggling to free themselves and coalesce into the emerging Baroque totality. The resultant tension is expressed in shoes that start to show bulging outer soles and all sorts

Figure 2.4. The Mannerist Sneaker's straps, mesh, and irregular composite sole

of Velcro straps, as if the shoe were agitated energy pushing outward and needing to be constrained. These animated shoe forms seem to be bursting their bounds as the Mannerist sneaker pulsates with energy and agitation.

Another example of the Mannerist sneaker style was the Charles Barkley[3] signature shoe (Figure 2.5), with its sense of agitated motion that dramatized constraining energy rather than becoming a manifestation of that energy. In the Baroque shoes to follow, the employment of rounded bulging outer soles, dramatic embroidered façades, and contrasting fields of light and dark color represent a more successful merger of energy and form. In the Mannerist sneaker, though, forms have not as yet developed to the extent that they can contain the new post-Classic sense of movement. As a result, the principal effect became one of dramatizing the constraint of energy.

The Barkley sneaker appears as a white inner shoe or sleeve covered with four sandal straps as if holding down the agitation beneath. The necessity of constraint to keep the composition from exploding is furthered by the presence of what appears to be strengthened eyelets (small plastic half-oil barrels) at the end of the four straps, such that tightening the laces is also pulling the straps tight. Furthermore, there are four elastic belts connecting right and left eyelets for an added effect of having to constrain an inner energy struggling to get out. The result of all these straps, belts, and reinforced eyelets is to create an effect of a very convulsive shoe that is bursting with energy and agitation. On the sides of the straps are scattered portholes with silver mesh windows and a touch or two of purple on the heel, all of which make no particular sense in terms of an overall design and just add to the crowded hodge-podge Mannerist effect. More agitation is added by what appears as white teeth stuck into the side of the outer sole, as if the shoe were the gum of some sort of sneaker jaw. With four teeth on one side and three on the other, it was a very contrived Mannerist effect. The teeth, though, are only on the front end of the shoe. At the back is the Nike air bubble supporting the heel. Teeth and bubble have no apparent reason to be combined in a single otherwise continuous sole.[4]

The Baroque Sneaker

Going into the 1990s the crowded and agitated tendencies associated with Mannerism give way to sneakers that are more massive and

Figure 2.5. The Mannerist Sneaker's teeth, straps, agitation, and sense of constrained energy (Photokaya)

colossal, emphasizing movement and a sense of the dramatic. Here the earlier tension of shoe elements resisting their assigned place is gone, as they are either fused together or dominated by one of them in a new wave of shoe styling that could be called the Baroque sneaker (see Figure 2.6).

A bulging sole. In art history the Baroque is defined by the sense of the massive and colossal as well as by constant movement. That weightiness becomes a dramatic effect when, for example, the columns of seventeenth-century Baroque churches bulge outward at their base to dramatize the colossal and massive. Such a Baroque effect is seen nowhere more clearly than in the oversized and outwardly bulging soles that appear in the 1990s as the sequel to the straight, relatively narrow, and elegant sole of the earlier Classic sneaker or to the discontinuous jumbled sole of the Mannerist sneaker. If one simply focuses on the sole of the shoe, the sequence is: chunky and solid in the Archaic; slender, elegant, and straight in the Classic; jumbled in the Mannerist; and oversized and bulging in the Baroque.

Earlier Archaic sneakers also felt weighty and somewhat massive, but that was derived from the effect of largely unstructured raw material comprising the thick rubber sole. But in the Baroque sneaker massiveness is an explicit design effect expressed through oversized and bulging soles as if responding to weight pressing downward. Here the earlier Classic lightness is now replaced by a sense of downward motion, weight, and seriousness. Accordingly, promotional material emphasized the domination, triumph, and victory that were to be gained by using these shoes on the basketball court. The earlier image of "Air" Jordan, the airborne figure of Michael Jordan floating above the basket to dunk the ball, is now replaced with the scowls and grim "game day faces" of professional athletes. For example, a Nike magazine ad for its "Air Zoom GP" shoe reads as follows.

EVERY GOOD POINT GUARD KNOWS

Lightning Kills,
the sudden strike, the unpredictable surge from spot to spot,
leaving defenders (we smell smoke) melted to the floor three feet
behind the play.
Let the word go forth to all defenders: Storm comin'.

Figure 2.6. The Baroque Sneaker's massive effect realized as bulging soles and constant movement (Photokaya)

With phrases like "lightning kills," "sudden strike," "unpredictable surge," "melted to the floor," and "storm comin'," this shoe is not about "air" but about power, force, and domination. The Baroque sense of movement is seen not only in the wavelike motion of the outer sole but also in its rounded edges as it curves beneath the shoe. It has been said that the Baroque abhors edges, boundaries, and sharp right angles, and this is nowhere more clear than in the soft flowing movement of the Baroque sneaker's sole, which is of such a rounded nature that decorative effects appear on the bottom of the sole, which is now part of the overall design package and accordingly is given its own shape and color (see Figure 2.7).

This rounding of the sole breaks down the overall contour line of the shoe, as the Baroque sneaker appears more and more a singular entity. The upper flows into the sole in continuous motion, and the side of the sole flows under to the bottom in one seamless movement of color, design, and decorative effects. From top to bottom it is a singularity. This can be seen in the two views of the same Baroque sneaker in Figure 2.6 and 2.7.

Eradicating the sole line. At the heart of Classic styling is the presence of clearly articulated subcomponents that are assembled with a variety of principles (proportion, balance, symmetry, and so forth). In general the most basic shoe division is between sole and upper, and with a waving sole line the independent existence of the upper and sole is threatened. When the outer sole's wavelike movement splashes up the side of the shoe[5] the integrity of the upper is now compromised (Figure 2.6), as the shoe appears less the union of two separate parts and more a single object. This distinction between upper and sole can also be masked by having the upper extend downward to cover parts of the sole, and in this configuration the shoe appears as a gigantic upper with no, or only a minimal, sole. This is usually done by extending the color of the upper onto the sole, as seen in Figure 2.8.

Embroidery, incomplete, and irregular forms. The Baroque commitment to moving forms is not limited to the sole. The decorative designs on the side of the upper shift from the simple and clear embroidery of 1980s High Classicism to a twisting, swirling, Celtic-like thicket of criss-crossing embroidery. In the Classic sneaker, form is expressed through a clean line that establishes the shoe's overall contour and

Figure 2.7. A Baroque Sneaker's continuation of design elements from the side to the bottom of the shoe

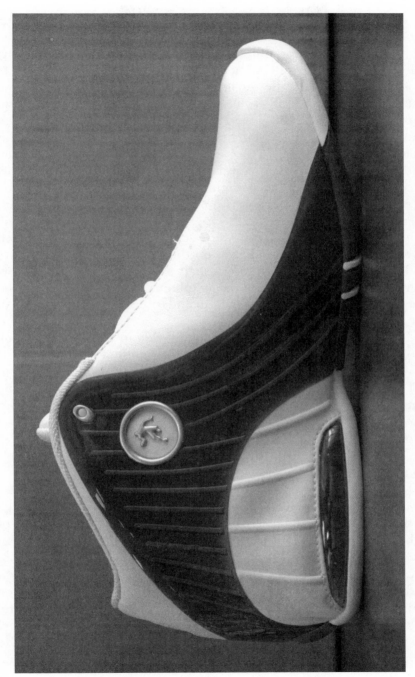

Figure 2.8. A Baroque Sneaker's fields of contrasting colors masking the line between the upper and the sole (Photokaya)

highlights the independent effects of heel, toe, and sole. In Baroque shoes, form appears as a swirling inner mass. There is no clear articulatory line. Line is now multiple lines, constantly stopping, starting, twisting, and turning, such that the eye cannot settle on any one line or form and has to settle for grasping the shoe as a whole. In the Baroque sneaker the wavy sole, swirls of embroidered stitchery, and maze of colorful markings zig-zagging across the surface created a blur of movement that kept the eye from centering on any particular element (see Figure 2.9). The eye just jumps back and forth between lines, forms, curves, and crossover embroidery, with no place to settle, except upon the shoe as a whole, which is precisely the Baroque effect. Classic design was based on symmetry. For every movement there was a countermovement. The Baroque is more asymmetrical, from the bottom of the shoe, where sculpted outer soles are carved one way on one side and another on the other; to the upper, where embroidered forms take different shapes on either side of the shoe. As with other Baroque effects, the asymmetry in decoration keeps the eye from settling on any one element and forces a comprehension of the complete design.

The asymmetrical effect can be clearly seen in Figure 2.10, which shows the heel of a Baroque sneaker. Start with the sole. The support air bubble goes about two-thirds of the way around the heel from left to right, then stops, and then we see only about a quarter of the remaining heel with the bubble. Moving upward we see a supporting cup of white material that tilts to the right and on top of that is another stitched piece that leans to the left while the remainder of the upper that is seen (with the black stripes) is disproportionately on the right-hand side.

Contrasting fields of color. Wolfflin argued that the clear contoured edge of figures in High Renaissance painting gave way to an interplay of light and dark as one of the design features of the Baroque. This can also be seen in sneakers, where shoe colors are emancipated from being confined in forms, as they were in Classic styling. Fields of light and dark color are now free to roam across the surface of the shoe without regard to its architectural structure. In the Classic shoe, the colors stayed within the form of the embroidered strips and acted principally as a line to articulate the heel, sole, toe, and eyelets. In the Baroque, color is free to cross over such components and constitute

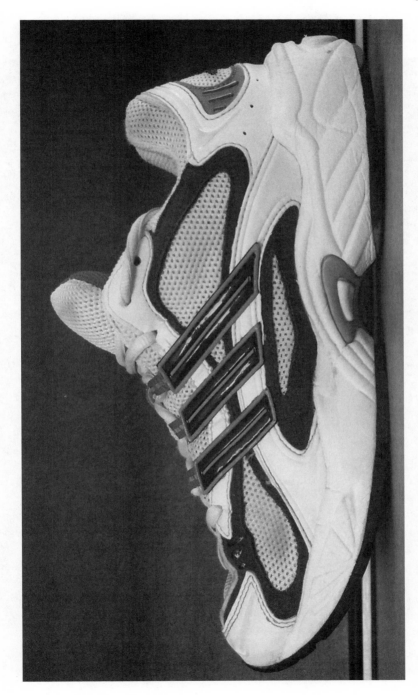

Figure 2.9. A Baroque Sneaker's cross-stitching effect to keep the eye from focusing upon one constituent shoe element

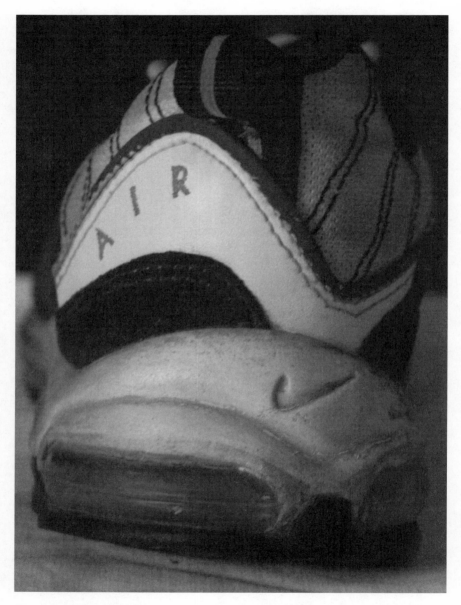

Figure 2.10. A Baroque Sneaker's irregular, unbalanced style effects

its own effect. Color is no longer limited to the supporting role of outlining forms. As seen in Figure 2.8, the main visual effect is the contrast between large fields of light and dark, which is not bounded by the shoe's subcomponents over which they roam.

When looking at this shoe, the eye bounces back and forth between the light and the dark, unable to settle on either. The dark color field covers part of the sole and part of the upper and obliterates the sole line dividing them, thus violating one of the central principles of the Classic style. The shoe no longer appears as a combination of an independent sole and an upper, but as the interplay of two free-floating fields of color. The shift from Classic to Baroque styling is the transition in feeling derived from apprehending the balance and proportion of a composition of self-contained elements to one of a basking in light and dark colors.

Façades. As a dramatic frontal piece attached to an underlying architectural form, a façade is traditionally seen on buildings, but it also appears in sneaker design. In buildings of the High Renaissance, the Classic principles of order and symmetry were manifest in the balanced composition of windows around a door or pediments above a window. In Baroque architecture, such balanced parts are played down in favor of a central effect, such as some kind of façade on the front of the building. If for the sake of analogy we consider the shoe in such architectural terms, then in Classic composition there is a balance among colors and articulated parts of the shoe, like the balance between windows, doors, and pediments in classically designed buildings. The equivalent of the addition of a façade on a building, then, is the addition of embroidered patches, embedded plastic nuggets, or elaborate stitchery patterns on the side of Baroque sneakers. In both building and sneaker, the façade effect is the same; it attracts the eye and constitutes a single dominant effect that reduces the importance of the other components, whether windows and doors or toes and heels.

The Rococo Sneaker

The 1990s trend toward solemn monumental sneakers with heavy bulging soles and large fields of primary colors declined at the turn of the century in favor of more delicate forms and fading pastel colors reminiscent of the eighteenth-century Rococo styling that followed the serious solemnity of the seventeenth-century Baroque. Stepping back and looking at the style cycle, there now appear to be two major style movements—Classicism and Baroque—and two minor, or transitional styles—Mannerism and Rococo. Mannerism appears at the end of the Classic phase, and Rococo at the end of the Baroque. Shoes with light pastel colors, vine-like welded plastic decorative lines wafting upward, cut-out holes to reveal an undergarment of mesh, and a reduction in the bulging sole all work toward dissolving the solidity and solemn massiveness of the Baroque shoe, and usher in the era of the Rococo sneaker.

Colors. At the end of the 1990s decorative effects began to change. Rather than the large sheets of solid primary colors (red, white, black, blue) that dominated Baroque sneaker design, there was a shift to pastels, which can be seen in the available colors for Nike's running and cross-training shoes: light bone, olive, grey, cool grey, neutral grey, grey haze, smoke, light graphite, blue chalk, celery, gold leaf, and heaven blue. Colors for basketball shoes were, by and large, still from the earlier period: white, black, midnight navy, deep garnet, varsity royal, and varsity red. But even here the Rococo effect can be seen, as basketball shoes can be found in light blue, metallic silver, and mustard yellow, colors unheard of in the older Baroque days when black and white schemes dominated. This introduction of pastel colors works against the sense of downward movement that was engendered with the darker primary colors of the Baroque era. The Baroque phase signaled not just weight but solemnity and seriousness, whereas the lighter Rococo pastels create a more casual and light-hearted effect.

Vine-like lines. In Rococo styling there is a rise in the importance of surface decoration at the expense of the shoe's more basic architectural features. In Wolfflinesque terminology, the Rococo sneaker spews its decorative effects across the surface of the sneaker, as accent lines begin to delicately crawl, creep, and drip over the shoe (see Figure 2.11).[6] With this there is also a rise in the importance of surface decoration at the expense of the shoe's more basic architectural features. Decorative accent lines, whether as sewn folds in the fabric of the upper or welded plastic on the wall of the shoe, are now thinner and do not articulate shoe components (as in the Classic shoe) nor dramatize the

Figure 2.11. The Rococo Sneaker's wavy, pastel-colored lines

massive and the colossal (as in the Baroque shoe). Such accent lines show two general patterns. First, they follow the traditional Rococo pattern of an "S-like" motif reminiscent of the gold gilded interior wall decorations in early eighteenth-century rooms. The "S" pattern can be seen in Figure 2.11.

Second, there is a general tendency toward lightness and ascendancy in both line and color intensity. Lines become thinner as they ascend the sides of the sneaker, and colors become lighter. All of these changes reinforce the status of the Rococo style as a more secondary art of decoration that follows the lead of a preexisting architectural form. The Baroque sneaker's effects were more architectural than decorative, with an emphasis on the grandeur of an enlarged and massive sole, an intense pattern of stitchery, and a seriousness of large fields of primary colors. If it could be said that the seventeenth-century Baroque placed more emphasis on the architectural exterior and the eighteenth-century Rococo upon decorating the interior, then by general analogy we can say that the 1990s Baroque sneaker was more concerned with the exterior public self involved in competitive group sports, whereas the turn-of-the-century Rococo sneaker dealt more with the private self of running and personal fitness.

The dissolving shoe. With thin vine-like movements of surface decoration, the solidity of the wall of the shoe appears to dissolve in the delicate flickering effects of the interplay of thin wavy lines and shifting pastel colors. Rococo lightness in sneakers is sometimes attained by the use of an outer shell that has large sections cut out, resulting in something of a "cage" that surrounds the inner shoe. The effect is as if the shoe wall had been cut away in a variety of ovals, rounded rectangles, triangles, and scalloped shapes, acting to deflate the solidity of the earlier Baroque shoe wall. In general, the size, shape, and degree of protrusion of the sole is more a style effect than a functional necessity. The crudely hewn rubber of the Converse All-Star generated the rough effect of the Archaic shoe, the narrow elegant sole of the first Air Jordan the Classic effect, and the teeth in the sole of the Barkley the Mannerist effect of dramatizing the energy that is later built into the waving soles of the Baroque shoe. Rococo soles are less massive and wavy than Baroque ones, as the forward section of the outer sole seems to be crumbling or eaten away by acid or corrosion, as if one is witnessing the sole dissolving in front of his or her eyes.

It is another technique used to lessen the solemnity of the previously massive Baroque style. When this effect is combined with a pastel-colored upper decorated with thin vine-like lines, the combined effect is of an almost disappearing shoe wall compared to the heavy and colossal Baroque shoe.

By the early twenty-first century the sneaker style cycle seemed to have come to an end. Following the Rococo sneaker, the styles seemed more pluralist, a mixture of retro rediscoveries of early models, often carried in sections of shoe stores called "classics," interestingly enough, and the appropriation of the sneaker by expensive traditional shoe manufacturers who began to bring out designer sneakers.

Theorizing the Style Cycle

If the style cycle has run its course, how are we to understand what has transpired? What, for instance, is the relationship between the life cycles of style found in ancient Greece, the Renaissance, and now sneakers? Given the surface similarity of these patterns, it would seem that Vasari identified a very robust cultural dynamic that can be observed in quite different historical periods. In the case of the Classic sneaker, it appeared during the 1970s and 1980s, which, some have suggested, was the start of a "great new athletic-cultural-commercial empire " (Halberstam 1999:131). Others have argued that a cabal of sneakers, endorsements, and American corporations created a "new global commercial power [where] ... the United States had come to command global financial power, communications systems, marketing networks, and cutting-edge technologies ... [and] Jordan [and those sneakers] exemplified this imperial control" (LeFeber 2002:14, 24). This was also the period at which the status value and prestige of the sneaker reached its peak.

If styles are independent of social questions of status, or commercial power, then the Classic sneaker could appear at any time. But it didn't. It did not appear during the early twentieth century when the modern sneaker was evolving, both in popularity and in commercial success. Nor has it lasted as a permanent style, and with the decline in the sneaker as a status object has come a style shift away from the Classic. Was that just an accident? Possibly. But if we examine the periods in which the Classic emerged in ancient Greece and in European painting, the historical record suggests that this style's appearance is associated with concentrations of power. The period of Athenian hegemonic influence was also the period of Classic forms of Greek art, and the height of power of the Holy Roman Empire and efforts at control over Europe by Charles V of Spain was also a period of the Classic High Renaissance style. To this we could add the commercial power of shoe companies and the status and prestige of the sneaker in world culture.

But why should a concentration of status and power correlate with a particular style of expression and, more specifically, why with the Classic style? The Gramscian answer, I think, is that power and principles of style have more than a spurious relationship. One serves the other. If one were to characterize hegemonic culture, it would probably include the notion that in essence it is a type of social control that has, at one and the same time, moral principles about the autonomy of the individual and their ordered configuration. I do not think it is an accident, therefore, that under moments of hegemonic power (from Athens to American commerce), principles of art with a mix of rules that govern constituent forms operate alongside another set of principles about the self-animating naturalism of these constituents.

The essence of the Classic style, then, is precisely the essence of the hegemonic mode of social control. The Classic became the visual realization of the Gramscian notion of hegemony, as rule by ideas, where here it is rule by principles of style. This is because Classic principles of balance and symmetry imply an ordering centerpoint around which said elements are placed, hence the implied order—the absent, yet present, hegemonic presence. So too with elegance. It seems strictly a matter of aesthetic judgment, yet it is a set of ordering principles that arrange artistic material—from marble in statuary to synthetic material and shoelaces in sneakers. At heart, elegance is a question of control: not to slop over borders, or be random or messy. To be poised is to be under control, such that a well-ordered social universe is one in which a Classic outlook probably prevails. Conversely, a social universe of change, disorder, revolt, and resistance is one in which things are less structured, balanced, or symmetrical.[7]

It is not an accident, then, that periods of concentrations of power, whether in Greek city-states, European nations, or contemporary global commerce, bring forth, or are manifestations of, principles of symmetry, balance, and harmony. With the passing of Athenian power came the passage of the Classic in Greek art; with the passing of Spanish-Habsburg power came the passage of High Renaissance Classicism in European art; and now, with the passing of the immense popularity, importance, and status of sneakers in youth culture came a shift away from the style hegemony of the Classic sneaker. During most of the twentieth century the sneaker was rising to prominence, in style, status, and commercial success; and that—not accidentally, I now think—was the period of the Archaic sneaker. Then for a short period there was a concentration of importance, status, and commercial success of the sneaker, and that was the period of the Classic sneaker. Finally, with the decline in the prestige and status of the sneaker in youth culture came the transition to the Baroque sneaker, followed by the Rococo style, whose lightness and frivolity marked the quiet end of the Sneaker Era.

Put this way, perhaps I have too quickly abandoned Vasari's life cycle model. Perhaps his model is exactly what we have observed over the twentieth century. The sneaker and its style were born, matured, and reached a classic elegance, to then decline in status, importance, and balanced composition. As we move into the twenty-first century, the time of the power, influence, and status of the sneaker seems increasingly one of an earlier era.

Notes

1. Wolfflin's writing is very powerful and seductive, and I find myself inadvertently using his words and phrases. I occasionally note my use of Wolfflinesque language, but I am sure there are more times that I have unconsciously used his words or phrases than I want to admit.

2. Examples of such agitated decoration include Reebok's "Kamikaze," with severe zig-zag lightning strikes across the shoe's side; Converse's "Voltage," with zig-zag stitching like a scrambled pattern on a television screen; and Nike's "Air Barrage Mid," which has bulging soles, a strap across the shoe's top, and "swoosh" logos overflowing the composition. Everything looks like it has been forced onto this shoe, making it the epitome of Mannerist styling.

3. Charles Barkley was a professional basketball player.

4. Another good example of Mannerist styling was the Magic Johnson signature shoe from Converse, which had the awkward look of a plastic ski boot, with different parts patched together like so much riveted boilerplate on a metal boot for a medieval knight. Each part of this sneaker stands out awkwardly, clearly bounded by obvious stitching that attaches each separate piece of shoe material. The separate pieces of the shoe reflect the Classic heritage of autonomous forms, and as such,

styled in the manner of earlier Classic designs. The difference is that the pieces are often oversized (the heel piece in particular) and so do no fit into an overall balanced design. Such exaggerated parts of a figure were characteristic of sixteenth-century Mannerist painting, as seen in the elongated neck and fingers of Parmigianino's *The Madonna with the Long Neck* (c. 1535) and the exaggerated size of the hand in his *Self Portrait* (1524). Compare the Johnson heel with the one on the Air Jordan I. The Jordan heel is part of the overall shoe, in both color and material. The Johnson heel stands apart from the shoe as a cup or hard container into which the rest of the shoe appears to be stepping. The shoe has purple, yellow, and grey accent marks scattered over the surface, but they do not point to, or contribute toward, realizing any particular effect; they seem random and arbitrary. Similarly, the sole is an amalgam of component materials and colors lacking in any clear purpose. Decoratively, the logo (CONS) is awkwardly tilted and placed not only on the shoe's side, like the Nike "swoosh" (✔) on the side of the Air Jordan I, but also on the heel and tongue, crowding the overall design with logos. There is also an unnecessary strap over the toe, a hallmark of Mannerist shoe design, which like the scattered logos, large heel cup, and randomly distributed purple/grey/yellow accent marks, does not appear part of any obvious design. It is as if nothing quite belongs in its place. All the elements seem separate, like the earlier Classic style, but not ordered into any elegant, proportional, or balanced composition.

5. In Nike's "Air Penny," for instance, the motion of the sole appears to splash almost to the top of the upper, making the sole and its continuation up the side of the shoe the dominant effect. The eye goes immediately there, and what's left (heel, laces, tongue, and toe) are all reduced to supporting effects at best. The opposite kind of effect can be seen in the "Air Jordan XIII," in which the black coloration of the upper seems to drip over the white sole, like fudge over chunks of vanilla ice cream, allowing only intermittent pieces of the sole to be seen. The "Air Jordan XIV" works similarly, whereby a constant white upper seems to continue right down and through the sole, making the shoe appear all upper. Although rising sole and descending upper are opposite designs, their effect is the same. The shoe is more of a single totality, whether as sole or upper. It is no longer a balanced composition of a separate and independent sole and upper.

6. In the Rococo sneaker, line shows much less purposeful direction, as can be seen in the almost random direction of lines on the side of the Nike "Tuned Swoops," "Air Terra Goatek," and "Air Max Plus" shoes.

7. These ideas of things in their place have roots in sociological theory as well as in art history. Durkheim (1965) and Mary Douglas (1966) classically articulated the relationship between a sense of social order and things being in their place. Some of these ideas we will return to in Chapter 3's discussion of different cultural logics for the social construction of monsters and mythical creatures in Eastern and Western civilization.

CHAPTER THREE

Rambo and Don Quixote
Cultural Icons of National Decline

CERVANTES'S NOVEL *DON QUIXOTE* (1605, 1615) and the two Vietnam War films starring Sylvester Stallone, *First Blood* (1982) and *Rambo* (1985), are rarely spoken of in the same breath. One is a great work of literature, the others popular culture rarely on any list of important cinema. Yet book and film share a number of similarities. First, they were not isolated texts but instances of more general cultural tempers. In the case of *Don Quixote* there were a number of parodies of romantic chivalry written at the same time (de Riquer 1981:901–903). As for *Rambo,* there were a number of films with similar themes of rescuing American prisoners of war (POWs) in the 1980s. The Sylvester Stallone film maybe the most famous, but it is not the only one on the topic.[1]

Second, both novel and film were internationally popular. There were four authorized editions of *Don Quixote,* and others came out in Milan and Brussels along with translations into French and English (Watt 1996:67). *Rambo* was not only watched in the United States but reportedly was the most popular film in Lebanon's history and the most popular video rental in Yugoslavia. Supposedly one-seventh of Iceland's population saw it during its first week (Warner 1992:688).

Third, both of these mythical characters became global images. The tall thin knight with tattered armor on broken steed, accompanied by a short squat squire, has been painted over the centuries by artists such as Hogarth, Fragonard, Daumier, Dore, Picasso, and Dali (Watt 1996:282). While the historical verdict on the permanence of the Rambo image remains to be seen, it is nonetheless amazing how widespread and popular the image of Rambo has become. It is a similarly clear-cut image: the muscle-bound commando fighter with a bandanna around his forehead, machine gun in his hand, and a strap of bullets over his shoulder.

Fourth, along with visual imagery the central theme of both novel and film have become part of world culture. The Merriam-Webster Online Dictionary defines *quixotic* as "foolishly impractical especially in the pursuit of ideals; *especially*: marked by rash lofty romantic ideas or extravagantly chivalrous action," while a Random House dictionary defines *Rambo* as "a fanatically militant or violently aggressive person [after John Rambo, a Vietnam veteran in the motion picture *First Blood* (1982) and its sequels]." As the term "quixotic" has entered the language, so has "Rambo." Oliver North, for instance, was compared to Rambo by some twenty columnists and commentators around the time of the Iran-Contra scandal (Warner 1992:686), while more recently the French interior minister Nicolas Sarkozy was referred to as having a "Rambo-like attitude" in his reaction to the 2005 riots that broke out in France.

Finally, they are both self-made caricatures. Don Quixote was an idle reader of books, and John Rambo in *First Blood* was a Vietnam vet who wandered the back roads of Oregon. What transforms them into "Don Quixote" and "Rambo" is their total self-absorption into the ways and ideals of a particular knightly and military creed, ethic, or worldview. These were not just literary escapes or memories, or even scars from war, but a set of ideas that had gripped them in such a way that it took over their existence in a way that led them to act as if it were then and they were knight-errant and Vietnam decorated Special Forces soldier.

Neither is the buffoonish character that will become part of our consciousness, for John Rambo doesn't start out as a living-off-the-land Special Forces soldier and Don Quixote doesn't have that particular name, nor armor, horse, lance, or squire. Both transform themselves into the tragic heroes the world would later recognize. Rambo takes off his shirt and fastens a warrior's cloak of sorts from a piece of discarded canvas and ties a bandanna around his forehead to keep his long hair from his eyes in the combat to come. Don Quixote takes up some old rusty armor and a lance, obtains a horse, and fashions a helmet visor. Both constitute their Special Forces/chivalrous knight identity out of tattered material and begin adventures none of their contemporaries think appropriate or reasonable. To seventeenth-century Spaniards, Don Quixote is mad; to twentieth-century Oregonians, Rambo is crazy.

First Blood

To see these points in somewhat more detail, I will begin by comparing the film *First Blood* (1982) with Cervantes's novel. These stories are not about royalty or people of high office. They begin with ordinary circumstances: Don Quixote is introduced as a poor hidalgo, a member of the lowest order of the Spanish nobility, and John Rambo first appears on screen as a regular soldier, a Vietnam veteran in jeans and combat boots wearing a surplus army coat and carrying a sleeping bag over his shoulder. There is also aimlessness to the beginning of their adventures. Prior to becoming Don Quixote, Alonso Quixano's life is spent reading escapist chivalry novels, whereas John Rambo is introduced to the audience wandering on foot down a dusty country back road to call on a fellow Vietnam veteran.

Alonso Quixano did nothing but read books of romantic chivalry. "In short, he became so absorbed in his books that he spent his nights from sunset to sunrise, and his days from dawn to dark, poring over them; and what with little sleep and much reading his brain shriveled up and he lost his wits. His imagination was stuffed with all he read in his books about enchantments, quarrels, battles, challenges, wounds, wooings, loves, agonies, and all sorts of impossible nonsense" (Cervantes 1981:26). John Rambo's imagination was filled with Vietnam War wounds and memories about quarrels, battles, challenges, loves, and agonies. If these sentiments had remained mere memories or fantasies, then, yes, they would have been considered out of step with the present and maybe even delusional, but they would not have become "Don Quixote" and "Rambo." Something else was required. They had to act upon those beliefs, and act they did.

The story begins when John Rambo, arrested as a vagrant in a small Oregon town, is roughed up by local sheriff's deputies. He goes on to escape, running into nearby mountains while being chased by these deputies. Right from the start the description of Don Quixote seems to fit Rambo: "As [*Don Quixote*] proceeds the complete alienation of its hero from his time and environment emerges more and more distinctly. He cannot and will not adapt himself to this world. Where others make themselves useful and fit in, he makes himself ridiculous, useless, actually harmful" (Hauser 1965:323). This is a perfect description of John Rambo. He does not fit into post–Vietnam War America. He makes himself not only useless and ridiculous but very harmful. Claiming he broke no laws and only came to town to get something to eat, Rambo says that in pushing him around the sheriff's deputies had drawn "first blood" and, in effect, since they had started the conflict, they would have to bring it to a close.

This is the quixotic premise: the ideal that causes such pain when reality is forced to meet its demands. Calling this Rambo's knightly honor is perhaps the wrong phrase—but his honor code, reflecting his status as a highly trained member of an elite military unit (the Green Berets), has been challenged. With a more realistic perspective he could have spent a few nights in jail, end of story. But his incident with the sheriff, plus his sense of honor, starts his adventure.

This code of honor is the first element of the Quixote-like "madness" of John Rambo: applying his set of firmly held ideals ("they started it, they drew first blood, they will have to stop it") in the wrong place at the wrong time. What might have served him as a source of courage and motivation in the military is now, as a civilian, a source of havoc and violence. Rambo follows his code, made for jungle military warfare, and applies it to civilians and volunteers, sheriff's deputies, National Guard weekend warriors, dads, and their sons, just as Quixote followed his code, made for earlier centuries of Spanish chivalry, and applied it to his fellow countrymen. Ideals in opposition to reality is the moral of both stories.

Ideals versus Reality

The dramatization of psychological ideals versus outer social reality begins on Don Quixote's first day of adventure when he comes to an inn for the night and proclaims that it is a castle.

> The moment he saw the inn he pictured it to himself as a castle with its four turrets and pinnacles of shining silver, not forgetting the drawbridge

and moat and every feature usually ascribed to such castles.... At the door were standing two young women, party girls as they call them [and] he perceived the two misguided damsels, who seemed to him to be two fair maidens or lovely ladies taking their ease at the castle gate.... At this moment it so happened that a swineherd who was going through the harvested fields collecting a drove of pigs ... gave a blast on his horn to bring them together. Forthwith it seemed to Don Quixote to be what he was expecting, the signal of some dwarf announcing his arrival. (Cervantes 1981:31)

In the movie *First Blood,* the first incident also begins with Rambo misinterpreting reality to conform to his state of mind. Taken to the sheriff's station for interrogation and booking and beaten for noncompliance, Rambo looks out the window and sees Vietnam. Not the reality that is small-town Oregon, but a delusion that appears as Vietnam where he had earlier been imprisoned. Don Quixote saw an inn as a castle; Rambo sees a sheriff's station as a Vietnamese prison camp. Don Quixote sees two young women as "fair maidens or lovely ladies"; John Rambo sees the approaching sheriff's deputy, who wants to give him a shave, as a Vietnamese army officer who wants to torture him with a gigantic knife. Don Quixote doesn't just inhabit one reality; he flips back and forth between his world in seventeenth-century Spain and the imaginary knightly time of Ferdinand and Isabella. And Rambo? He does the same thing, alternating between being imprisoned during the Vietnam War and being in a sheriff's office. After he escapes, he acts at times like a Special Forces operative fighting behind enemy lines and at others as someone in present-day Oregon.

Don Quixote and Rambo, then, psychologically live in worlds of make-believe knights and Special Forces soldiers who, from their distorted point of view, see ordinary citizens as either fellow knights waiting to be challenged or as combat soldiers seeking military engagement. John Rambo acts like he is again a Special Forces operative behind enemy lines. But it is all in his mind. He is, in reality, in the woods of Oregon, not in the jungles of Vietnam. While evading pursuers he surprises a teenager. Rambo raises his knife to kill the teen as if he were a Vietnamese combat soldier. But he freezes, looks at the boy, and realizes it is an American teenager, not a Vietnamese soldier. He lowers his knife and runs away into the woods. The Vietnam Special Forces code—finish the fight, survive at all costs, and don't quit—is now, away from Vietnam, in Oregon, creating havoc. Rambo almost killed a teenage boy.

In this quixotic universe, Rambo cannot tell which reality he is involved in: is it Vietnam, or Oregon? He treats Oregon local law enforcement like the North Vietnamese army; he employs all his Special Forces tricks, acting as if he is living off the land after having somehow parachuted behind enemy lines. He carves a stick to spear a wild pig to feed himself, and makes weapons from other sharp sticks to use against the sheriff's deputies. He runs, hides, and ambushes his civilian pursuers, disappearing and reappearing as though he were a stealth-like Special Forces soldier in the heat of combat. But John Rambo is really in Oregon. No war. No North Vietnamese regulars. No Special Forces operative. He is a veteran of a war that is now over. But not in his mind.

Don Quixote would understand Rambo's state of mind perfectly, for he had similar delusions. He viewed an advancing cloud of dust as an army (it was a herd of sheep). He charged that army, but he really charged sheep, wounding many. He would charge other knights, but he would really charge a monk and a barber by mistake. He saw a windmill and thought it was a giant. He charged the giant, but he really charged a windmill whose sail knocked him off his horse and sent him tumbling to the ground. Don Quixote thought he was a medieval knight—he wasn't. John Rambo thought he was a Special Forces operative—he wasn't.

"Cervantes' ambivalence towards chivalry is rooted in the inner contradiction ... between giving unqualified approval either to unworldly idealism or to worldly common sense [that] underlies the whole conception of the figure of Don Quixote and the whole psychology of the novel" (Hauser 1965:322). So too with the psychology of John Rambo, who is possessed with an unworldly idealism: continue the fight to the end, at any cost. "Don Quixote's tragedy is that of abstract idealism. The blind and uncompromising nature of what Ibsen calls the 'ideal demands,' and the obstinacy with which he maintains his 'so much the worse for the facts' attitude even after his most severe defeats by reality, permit no hope of his conversion to understanding and tolerance" (Hauser 1965:318). This is John Rambo's tragedy as well. For Rambo it is so much the worse for the people he encounters in the mountains of Oregon.

The Reality Principle

As with Quixote, there are attempts to convert Rambo to reality, and they come in the role of Rambo's old commander from Vietnam, Colonel Trautman, played by Richard Crenna. Trautman is called in to try to persuade Rambo to quit the fight. If Rambo is Quixote-like, then Colonel Trautman is Sancho Panza–like, for the Panza/Trautman characters are the material embodiments of the realist opposition to the idealist Quixote/Rambo worldview. Trautman, as the voice of reality, sharpens Rambo's quixotic character by playing the role played centuries earlier by Sancho Panza.

When Don Quixote sees windmills as giants, Panza asks, "What giants?" And when Rambo doesn't seem to realize he is outnumbered by the National Guard and sheriff's deputies, Trautman barks in a Panza-like fashion, "Look at 'em out there." Sancho Panza gets more specific: "Look, your worship. . . . What we see there are not giants but windmills" (Cervantes 1981:59); and later Trautman gets very specific in reminding Rambo of the reality of his situation: "Perimeters covered, no exits, nearly 200 men out there and a lot of M-16s. . . . This mission is over, do you understand me!" Don Quixote does not automatically give up his delusions when confronted with Sancho Panza's reality checks: "It's easy to see . . . that you are not used to the business of adventures. Those are giants" (Cervantes 1981:51). John Rambo also resists reality when Colonel Trautman tells him, "We can't have you running around wasting friendly civilians." Rambo answers, "There aren't any friendly civilians." Trautman tells him to quit. Rambo answers, "Nothing is over, you just don't quit!" This is the chivalric code of the military man.

Sometimes Trautman's reality position gets through to Rambo; most often it doesn't. For instance, he reaches him on a portable telephone in a cave where Rambo is hiding. A state policeman tries to communicate first: "State police calling John Rambo; acknowledge." Rambo says nothing, as if the reality of the world of the state police doesn't register, or will not be acknowledged. Then Colonel Trautman tries, and speaks in the two realities Rambo's quixotic mind flips back and forth between. "Company leader calling Raven," as if they were speaking in code on a mission back in the jungles of Vietnam. "Company leader to identify Baker team: Rambo, Meissner, Ortega,

Colleta, Jorgenson, Danforth, Barry, Krackower, confirm." Rambo now responds as if he were back in Vietnam: "They're all gone, sir. . . . Baker team, they're all dead. I am the last one, sir." In a quixotic shift, Trautman then returns to the present day: "Look, John, you've done some damage here. They don't want anymore trouble." Analogously, Sancho Panza asks Don Quixote about returning home when the adventure is going bad: "The best and wisest thing ... would be for us to return home" (Cervantes 1981:118). Trautman offers a similar suggestion to Rambo: flying him to Fort Bragg, North Carolina. After Rambo complains of being pushed around by the sheriff, Trautman gets frustrated and replies: "You did some pushing of your own." Confronted at this point with a reality check that he is, in fact, causing unnecessary violence, Rambo responds with his code of honor: "They drew first blood, not me." Then, staring into the campfire he started in his cave, he repeats softly, "They drew first blood," and then looks down into the flickering flames and is eerily quiet. The camera pulls back, revealing Rambo, alone, in his own Platonic cave, with the flickering fire reflecting off the cave walls, as a metaphoric representation of his entrapment within his honor code.

At this point Rambo's tragedy becomes clear. He is following a code of honor that is not applicable to the present situation: he has, therefore, reproduced the classic quixotic ideals-versus-reality gap. No matter what reality, Trautman points out, Rambo will not abandon his code of honor. He will stick by his soldierly ideals just as Don Quixote clung to his knightly views even when Sancho Panza points out the reality of the situation. "Sancho did not believe in what his Master believed, but he believed in his Master" (Leys 1998:34), and Colonel Trautman, Rambo's commanding officer in Vietnam, did not believe what Rambo believed either, but he believed in him. When the sheriff asks about Rambo, Trautman says he made him: "Rambo was the best." He was trained to ignore pain, weather, everything. His job was to kill—period. Rambo now fights his way back to town and nearly destroys it, setting fire to a gasoline station, igniting weapons in a gun store, and shooting out lights, signs, and windows of buildings, including the sheriff's office where his adventure began. The hellish scene of the town afire at night brings to a head the destructive consequences of the "they-started-it-they-will-have-to-quit-first" honor code. No matter what the reality, Rambo will not stop.

This willful attempt to bend reality to a set of ideals has created nothing but a burning inferno, and though Rambo seems successful, in the end he, like Don Quixote, is defeated and the code is relinquished. For Don Quixote the end came in a duel with the Knight of the White Moon, prior to which he stated that if he lost he would retire for a year and go home. He did lose and then went home, whereupon he announced that the spell was broken and that he was not Don Quixote but simply Alonso Quixano. "My good friends, I have happy news for you; I am no longer Don Quixote de La Mancha, but Alonso Quixano." Reality will not be bent to the chivalric will of Don Quixote, and it triumphs in the end.

The same fate now awaits Rambo. Reality eventually triumphs, and his spell is broken too. Having demolished the town, the sheriff's station, and triumphantly having the wounded sheriff at his mercy, Rambo encounters the reality principle again in the form of Colonel Trautman, who now joins Rambo in the destroyed sheriff's station. Heavily armed law enforcement officers have now encircled Rambo, and he is clearly outnumbered when the voice of reality appears in the form of his old commander. Colonel Trautman is adamant. He barks: "This mission is over, Rambo!" With reality bearing down, Rambo's psychic state is coming undone; the spell of the honor code, of continuing the fight to end, of never quitting, is about to collapse. Cornered and threatened, Rambo barks back, "Nothing is over, you just don't quit!" But things are starting to unravel psychically. He repeats his version of the modern chivalric knightly code and gets to the quixotic heart of the film.

"In the field we had a code of honor. Back here I can't hold a job."[2] Rambo is now clearly frustrated and breaking down. Worn out holding on to his honor code, he starts to quiver and shake as his speech rambles; he lashes out about how he can't get a buddy's death out of his mind. The quixotic spell finally releases its grip, and sitting on the floor he starts to cry like a baby while hugging Trautman. It's over. The spell is broken. In a scene dramatizing the triumph of reality, Trautman leads a handcuffed, head-down, clearly defeated Rambo out of the building.

Rambo

Although the first movie contained many quixotic elements, it was the sequel, *Rambo* (1985), featuring John Rambo as a one-man army performing unbelievable feats, that generated worldwide attention.

It is here that Rambo's ideals are most chivalrous, for his quest is to rescue the weak and defenseless: not damsels in distress, but missing-in-action Americans held as prisoners of war in Vietnam. On this quest Rambo was never more chivalrous, never more overdrawn, never more absurd, and never more the object of laughter:

> *Rambo* ... is at once hilarious and disgusting. It's hard not to howl at Stallone's ape-ish ambition.... It is to laugh when Stallone slaughters whole battalions of Vietnamese and Soviet soldiers.... It is even worth a chuckle when Stallone finally manages to grunt out a complete prepositional clause ("for our country to love us as much as we love it") in the closing thirty seconds. (Kopkind 1985:777)
>
> This sort of behavior becomes so comic that *Rambo* turns into something of a camp classic. (Canby 1985:C23)

This well-known public perception of the film as absurd, silly, and totally unreal makes its comparison with the novel possible. Great critical pride has been taken in pronouncing the unreality of Rambo's activities (see the movie critics' quotes above). Interestingly, though, I don't think critics went to great lengths pointing out how absurd it was for a man to joust with a windmill. Somehow the ideal/reality gap as an intellectual premise was granted to the novel but not, as far as I can tell, to the film. It is ironic, but all the criticism and dismissive comment on the Rambo films actually helps to make the point about its deeply quixotic nature.

In this film Rambo is offered an exit from prison (for his violent activities in *First Blood*) if he will go on a mission to Vietnam to look for, and photograph if found, American prisoners of war. He agrees. Rambo seems more inward, quiet, and moody than ever before. He appears emotionally wounded and deeply suspicious, emotions that reflect a sense of betrayal by a country that does not live up to its values and principles. Going into Vietnam to rescue the defenseless South Vietnamese from the more powerful aggressors from the North, which was the official explanation, could almost be conceived as a modern act of, if not national chivalry, then something at least very honorable. And if not honorable, it is at least the embodiment of a global power's justification to intervene around the world. As such, Rambo is imbued with a double dose of chivalry: first he was part of the earlier quest to save the South Vietnamese, and now he is out to rescue imprisoned and powerless prisoners of war. But the reality of the once-chivalrous nation that went into Vietnam has now changed, for there is no interest in going back to search for, or rescue, prisoners of war. Again the quixotic gap. Ideal: no soldier is left behind. Reality: the U.S. government doesn't want to upset the present geopolitical situation by sending search parties to Vietnam.

This new reality is embodied in Murdoch, the civilian government employee in charge of the mission to "recon for POWs in Nam." The physical contrast between Murdoch and Rambo is clearly drawn. In short-sleeved dress shirt and tie, Murdoch can't stand the heat of Asia and constantly drinks Coke for relief, whereas the tanned Rambo thrives in Asia's hot jungles. Don Quixote's quest was treated with ridicule; so was Rambo's. Murdoch is contemptuous at what Rambo wants to do, laughing at his attitude and concern for finding real POWs. He tells him the long and short of it is that he is "expendable," and his quest is out of place with the new political realities.

The story gives John Rambo thirty-six hours to look for POWs. If they are found, he must photograph them. But Rambo is not to engage the enemy. However, the U.S. government never thought there were POWs at this particular camp in the first place; the mission was a deceit, a cover to provide photos for a congressional committee to satisfy those who are still clamoring to find America's missing in action. Rambo, though, does find American prisoners and brings one back to the pick-up site, whereupon Murdoch, when he hears of this, orders the pick-up mission aborted. Reality and ideals clash.

The post–Vietnam War American political reality was not to engage the Vietnamese but to simply photograph POWs. The soldier's chivalric creed stood in opposition to both realities: It said, engage the enemy and rescue the prisoners. In *Don Quixote* the gap between ideals and reality was dramatized by the fact that those being rescued did not need to be rescued at all. In fact, Don Quixote's rescue efforts did more harm than good and made the knight look like a fool. For instance, he came across a man beating a boy and ordered him to stop. The man did, temporarily, but when Don Quixote left, the man, angered at someone interfering in his business, began to hit the boy even harder. A quixotic rescue does more hard than good.

The same holds for Rambo trying to rescue prisoners of war in Vietnam. Again, the very fact that the film was not taken seriously—that Rambo's rescue seems cartoonish, mythical, and absurd—is, in fact, the very grounds that makes it a quixotic statement. Don Quixote was also laughed at, and, importantly, if he had seen things as they were, if he properly calculated the odds before engaging in a fight or joust, he wouldn't be Don Quixote. The same is true of Rambo: if he didn't think he was a one-man army and didn't take on everyone, he wouldn't be Rambo. The gap between ideals (medieval chivalry) and reality (seventeenth-century Spain) is admittedly greater for Don Quixote than between Vietnam War and postwar history for Rambo, but the ideal/reality gap is the same and the moral backbone of both novel and film.

Violence

Rambo was criticized for its violence, but it is helpful to remember that this had also been a criticism of *Don Quixote*. Vladimir Nabokov's biographer said that "he detested the belly laughs Cervantes wanted his readers to derive from his hero's discomfiture.... [Nabokov's] distaste for Cervantes's sadistic treatment of Don Quixote reached such a point that he eventually excluded the book from his regular lectures on foreign literature at Cornell" (quoted in Leys 1998:33). It is interesting how similar Rambo and Don Quixote are in terms of the violence they inflict on others and on themselves, and how much critics commented upon this.

Don Quixote lost teeth and suffered endless stonings, beatings, falls, and battle wounds, whereas Rambo was tortured, shot at, wounded, slapped, struck, and cut with a knife. The cinematic reality has made the violence in the Rambo films a subject of much discussion, but if what occurred in *Don Quixote* was also realistically screened it too might have generated a Rambo-like reaction from critics. Consider, for example, the following scene. After his first day searching for adventure, Don Quixote stops at an inn for the evening. His armor is taken off and laid on a water trough. Later, a traveling mule driver attempts to move the armor from its resting place so he can water his mules. Having already attacked a previous mule driver for attempting the same thing, "Don Quixote, without uttering a word imploring aid from anyone, once more dropped his shield and once more lifted his lance. Without actually smashing the second driver's head to bits, he made more than three pieces of it, for he laid it open in four quarters" (Cervantes

1981:36). Imagine how that would look in full Ramboesque color on the wide screen.[3]

The film has also been faulted for a lack of conscience or feeling in the execution of Rambo's violence, as he certainly shows no regret when slaying any number of Vietnamese or Russian soldiers. Interestingly enough, a similar observation has been made about Don Quixote. "There is, then, very little of problem or tragedy in Cervantes' book.... Don Quijote's *idee fixe* saves him from feeling responsible for the harm he does.... Everything comes out all right, and time and again the damage done or suffered by Don Quijote is treated with stoic humor as a matter of comic confusion" (Auerbach 1969:110). Struck, wounded, and tortured numerous times, Rambo rarely uttered a peep and showed the most stoic demeanor. What Don Quixote said of himself could certainly have been said by Rambo. "If I make no complaint of the pain it is because knights-errant are not permitted to complain of any wound, even though their bowels be coming out through it" (quoted in Mancing 1982:50).

While critics have taken the film to task for its violence, it is important to remember that Rambo's desire to get even and seek revenge is most viscerally directed toward the Americans who sent him on his mission. Violence toward the Asian and Russian "Other" is clearly more wooden and comic book–like in character. The contradiction between Rambo's ideals (bring home the POWs) and Murdoch as the embodiment of reality (the war is over, there are no POWs) generates the most expressive anger in the film. When Rambo escapes his captors, he and the POWs he has freed head back to the base camp from which Murdoch sent him on his mission. Rambo radios from a helicopter that he is coming in with the prisoners of war he has rescued. Murdoch responds with a look of dread. Rambo then lands, jumps out, grabs a machine gun, and heads for the hanger that is Murdoch's office and operations headquarters. Firing the gun at all the computer and telecommunications equipment, he levels everything in sight. Then, with a scream, he drops the gun and confronts Murdoch, throwing him down on a table and raising his knife above his head as if to strike him. But instead, Rambo slams the knife's point into the table, barely missing Murdoch's head, as he yells "Mission accomplished!" He then repeats the "no man is left behind" chivalrous creed: "You know there are more men out there; find 'em or I'll find you." It is the most emotion shown in the whole film: American against

American, American ideals versus American reality. The quest is now over. Rambo wanders off into the distance. End of film.

> He chose to follow what would appear as the most absurd and impractical path: he followed the way of a knight errant in a world where chivalry had disappeared ages ago. Therefore clever wits all laughed at his folly. But in this long fight, which pitted the lonely knight … against the world, which side finally was befogged in illusion? The world that mocked them has turned to dust, whereas Don Quixote and Sancho live forever. (Leys 1998:34)

I don't know if this movie will have as long a life as *Don Quixote*. But I do believe that long after the world that mocked *Rambo* has turned to dust, Rambo the metaphor will live on. Few shallow films will have that kind of impact.[4]

Comparative Sociology of Literature

Given these similarities between Rambo and Don Quixote, what might they suggest about a comparative sociology of literature? Perhaps a hint is provided by the art historian Arnold Hauser, who suggested that "the tragedy of the individual knight is repeated on a wider scale in the fate of the chivalrous nation par excellence (1959, vol. 2:145). From a sociology of culture perspective, we might reverse Hauser's causal reasoning: perhaps it was the geopolitical fate of Spain that is mirrored in the tragedy of the individual knight. Let me quote Hauser again:

> For in spite of their victories and their treasures, the Spaniards had ultimately to yield to the economically more progressive Dutch and the more realistically minded British pirates. Even the war-tired heroes of Spain were no longer able to support themselves, and the proud hidalgo was reduced to penury, to the life of the rogue and vagabond. The chivalrous romance was indeed the least suitable preparation for the civil life that awaited the returning warrior. (Hauser 1965:320)

Again, one thinks of John Rambo. Home from the Vietnam War, unemployed, and wandering the back roads of Oregon, his honor code was indeed the least suitable preparation for the civil life that awaited the returning Special Forces warrior.

Is there, actually, support for a working hypothesis that links the beginning of Spanish decline and the appearance of *Don Quixote*? Although the timing of Spanish national decline is debated, there is support for the late sixteenth and early seventeenth centuries (Kindle-berger 1996:72), which, importantly, corresponds with the original publication of *Don Quixote* in 1605. A more systematic examination of statistical data on the size and strength of European armies and navies suggests a similar conclusion. "The first peak in the series, that of Spain, is reached in the late 1560s. Spanish decline then continued more or less through 1800" (Rasler and Thompson 1994:34). This conclusion is similar to that of Dehio (1962), who estimated Spanish Habsburg power to have peaked in 1585, as well as to that of Wallerstein (1974:165), who argued, "The Habsburgs under Charles V made a valiant attempt to absorb all of Europe into itself. By 1557, the attempt had failed. And Spain steadily lost not only its political imperium but its economic centrality as well."

> The wars of conquest in Italy, the victories over France, the fabulous colonization of America and the exploitation of its riches, had automatically become powerful propaganda for the military caste. Consequently it was here that the resurrected spirit of chivalry shone most brightly and disappointment was most bitter when its virtues turned out in practice to be obsolete. Nowhere else was the conflict between ideal and reality so acute, and nowhere was the disillusionment so great. (Hauser 1965: 320)

If Spain could be said to be living beyond its time, the same could be said of Cervantes's fictional creation Don Quixote, who maintained an outlook on life that was past its moment of relevance.

But how general is such an argument? Does it also hold for the United States and Rambo? Perhaps. There is some consensus within the world-system literature that American decline in the world economy showed signs of beginning in the 1970s,[5] and the Rambo films appeared shortly thereafter, in the 1980s. Like Spain before, the United States was now facing its own set of more competitive economies, this time from East Asia. Both Spain and the United States had also been involved in international moral crusades. Spain had taken the lead role in opposing Protestantism in Europe and Islam in the Mediterranean, both, from the point of view of Catholic Spain, highly moral if not chivalrous tasks.[6] The United States had also been the leading opponent of an ideological movement in the late twentieth century, international communism. This too was a moral crusade, with chivalric elements taking the form of ideas about standing up to communism, and coming to the aid of weaker countries, a logic that was used to legitimate American participation in the Vietnam War. Losing the Vietnam War, then, came as a particularly significant symbolic shock. With the protests against the war at home, the withdrawal signaled that the world was changing; it was to be the end of American enthusiasm for anticommunist military interventions. The world was clearly changing, for after the war it became increasingly apparent that the more efficient economies of Asia were coming to pose a particular threat to what had been U.S. economic preeminence.

Both Spain and the United States were on the cusp of a shift in international status. Foreign competition was rising; moral crusades were declining, and the moral superiority and their taken-for-granted centrality in the world-system was becoming ever more problematic. It is in that environment on the geopolitical plane that we see the emergence of works of art that dramatize the outdated nature of the ethics representative of the earlier sense of international superiority. What worked before, now the worldview of Don Quixote and John Rambo, was not working anymore.

If a chivalric code, or a Special Forces sense of honor, serves as a collective representation of the better days of the Spanish Empire and U.S. Cold War hegemony, then when there is slippage on the material plane it seems reasonable as a working hypothesis that dramas about a past hegemonic outlook that no longer works would be produced. There is no better way to dramatize American decline, or the disjuncture between the world of clear-cut U.S. military hegemony and an increasingly multicentric world, than by taking the symbolic representation of hegemonic prowess (Rambo and his code) and show it to be outdated, irrelevant, and downright destructive. Rambo acted as if he were fighting the Vietnam War, when he was in fact on American soil engaging weekend National Guard volunteers and the local sheriff department's bumbling deputies. Don Quixote engaged sheepherders, a barber, and others in a similar quest clearly out of touch with reality. Totemically, the message was the passing of the time of the chivalrous knight and the Special Forces operative; what was collectively represented was the passing of the national power and prominence of the nations for which these characters served as metaphoric representations.

Global Cultural Dynamics

There appear to be international cycles in both the political and economic spheres of the modern world, where most research has focused.[7] There has, though, been little research on cycles or pulsations of world-systemic cultural patterns,[8] but it stands to reason that if the political and economic spheres of the world-system pulsate or cycle, then perhaps the cultural sphere does as well. As a working hypothesis, let us assume that there are a variety of such global cultural cycles or repeating patterns of form and content that are clearly international in scope, and further, that *Don Quixote* and *Rambo* may very well be representations of such dynamics. What sort of cultural dynamic might these internationally popular cultural texts represent? Much of what they are about is no doubt unique to their authors, their national locale of production, and their historical period. I am not arguing that these are identical texts, but I want to suggest that their similarities do point toward some possible repetitive global cultural dynamics.[9]

First, the ideal/reality gap discussed earlier as the heart of Don Quixote and the Rambo films may actually have a geopolitical origin in the early moments of hegemonic decline. What we may have uncovered here is the world-systemic gap between hegemonic ideals and hegemonic decline, that the rise and fall of hegemonic states produces something like a quixotic/Ramboesque thematic. It will be incarnated in the historically contingent form of cultural expression of each historical period. As long as there is a world-system within which dominant states rise and fall, there will probably be gaps between past hegemonic ideals and present realities of decline that generate literature with a quixotic/Ramboesque quality.

The process here might be quite general. For periods of hegemonic ascent, it may be that the ideal reach may not exceed the material grasp. Rising states actually claim less than they could. The global cultural lag here works in the opposite direction. So, for example, in the nineteenth century, American art focused more on the safe and concrete in landscape painting. Given the actual growth of the U.S. economy, the artistic reach and claims could probably have been greater than they were. So, on ascent, countries tend to understate ideal claims. Then, given hegemonic prominence, there is a balance between ideals and material base. Things seem natural and appropriate. There is no gap. Neither the ascension gap of less idealism in thematic claims and narrative substance than their rising material base would actually warrant, nor the gap on the decline side where the ideals are too strong for the materiality of the past dominant nation now commencing decline. The downside produces the famed quixotic effect and charges of Ramboism. Muscularity devoid of material base; lashing out; violence without apparent reason; and most famously, actors acting on the basis of a hegemonic code, which is what chivalry is, when the material base of that hegemonic dominance is dissipating. For what is chivalry after all, but action without immediate material reason? And who can do that? Only the powerful; and on a national scale, only the hegemonic. Most human action is motivated by the baser motives: to eat, to seek revenge, to be frightened, and so forth. But to act for the larger good in a diffuse moral way, to save the weak for no reason but the sake of saving the weak, is a *noblesse oblige* mindset that is historically associated with the power and position of rank. Retheorize societal rank internationally and you have world-system position; and at the top you have hegemonic position.

When the material basis of the hegemonic nation and its chivalrous action begins to slip away, whether with the defeat of the Spanish Armada in 1588 or the U.S. defeat in the Vietnam War in the mid-1970s, it may not be an accident that people who had been witnesses to such highly symbolic national disasters would go on to compose works of expressive art wherein an individual stands in for the previously fully and unconsciously powerful nation. The code of the hegemon, the chivalrous code of international ranked position, is not "chivalrous" at all, but humorous, ridiculous—and worse, dysfunctional for and even violent to those whom it touches. It is about senseless violence to those who carry the code (Rambo and Don Quixote), and to all the other collateral others who get in the way of the dated moral code, forcing reality to meet its needs. The specifics of nation, history, and mode of expression (novel and film) change, but global dynamics remain, and as long as there is an international system with rising and falling hegemonic states, with their consequences for the people of the world, there will always be a resonance in world culture for quixotic themes and charges of Ramboism.

Why were these cultural products so popular? Great art? Perhaps in the case of *Don Quixote*. But their metaphoric residue (concepts of the quixotic and Ramboesque) have lived on past the immediate circumstances of their production. As such, it seems reasonable that they must have stood for something that audiences throughout the world understood. They have, among other things, captured the geopolitical sense of the cusp of decline, that false muscularity or bravado masking uncertainty, that appears when hegemonic ideals lag while the material base declines. It would seem, then, that as long as there is a world-system there will be moments of hegemonic decline and with that, at the beginning of that, moments when it is clear that there is a cultural lag between past hegemonic ideals and present realities. It was captured in *Don Quixote*, and the concept of the *quixotic* outlived both the experience of Spain and the salience of the novel. It appeared again, this time in film, in *Rambo*, and as before the concept at its core, *Ramboesque*, *Rambo-like*, and so on, outlived the salience of a 1980s movie.

Everyone knows that a realistic person doesn't joust windmills or take on armies. If he does, it is either a mistake, which is soon ruled out when he does it again and again, or he is mad, which is always hinted, but everyone knows mental illness isn't the point of novel or film. No, the culprit is outlook, creed, ethic, or code of honor, and furthermore everyone knows that it is a metaphor for the country, or once generalized, for persons or countries that act as they were when they are no longer.

Notes

1. Chuck Norris starred in *Missing in Action* (1984) as Special Forces colonel James Braddock, who returns to Vietnam to search for POWs. There was also a sequel, *Missing in Action 2: The Beginning* (1985), and in *Uncommon Valor* (1983) Braddock searches for his son. In *P.O.W.: The Escape* (1986), David Carradine's character goes behind enemy lines to bring back a group of American prisoners of war from Vietnam.

2. Ironically, the life of Cervantes shares some similarities with that of John Rambo. Cervantes came from a destitute family of the knightly aristocracy and was forced to serve as a common soldier because of his poverty. Wounded in battle during the Italian Campaign against the Ottoman Empire, Cervantes was taken prisoner by

Algerian pirates on his way home, and after many efforts at escape was released after five years in 1580. Back home in Spain he finds his family has fallen into poverty and debt. Further, there is no job awaiting him even though he is a hero of the Battle of Lepanto and a Christian knight who had been taken prisoner by what were considered heathens (Muslims). For all this he gets only a minor job as a tax-collector, suffers marriage problems, is imprisoned for a short time on a small offense, and witnesses Spain's humiliating defeat of its Armada to the British in 1588. After the Vietnam War Rambo said, "For me civilian life is nothing.... Back there I was in charge of million-dollar equipment. Here I can't hold a job." Cervantes might have said the same thing after the Battle of Lepanto.

3. This is not an isolated scene. In part one, book one, chapter four, Don Quixote stops a group of merchants and demands acknowledgment of the beauty of Dulcinea, and a muleteer takes Don Quixote's broken lance and begins to beat him until he is too weary to get up. In chapter eight, Don Quixote charges a monk on a mule whom he has confused for someone else. The monk escapes death by jumping off his mule. During this same time, Sancho Panza is being beaten by two muleteers. Don Quixote also challenges a gentleman squire from Biscay and wins the duel by hitting him with a very hard blow. Later in part one Don Quixote and Sancho Panza are beaten so badly by men accompanying a herd of horses that the men flee to avoid being charged with murder. The knight and his squire are not murdered but are too sore to move, and only after some time are well enough to limp to an inn. In chapter two, the knight imagines a maid to have been the daughter of the lord of the castle and to have fallen in love with him. After making advances, he is hit in the jaw and then trampled by a muleteer. In chapter three, a police officer arrives, whom Don Quixote wrongly insults as the cause of the trouble, and the policeman hits him with a lamp. In chapter four, mistakenly interpreting an approaching cloud of dust as an army, Don Quixote charges a herd of sheep, wounding many. The shepherds react and bombard Don Quixote with stones shot from slingshots, knocking him unconscious. In chapter five, Don Quixote encounters a funeral party and attacks a man who had shouted at him, and in chapter seven he mistakes a barber for a knight and charges him with his lance. The barber jumps off his horse to keep from being lanced. "Don Quixote turned into what he so often seems to be, that is, nothing but a dangerous visionary and madman" (Hauser 1965:319)—something close to the prevailing interpretation of Rambo, it would seem.

4. There was a third movie, *Rambo III* (1988), in which Rambo rescues Trautman from Russians who were holding him prisoner in Afghanistan. But there is no quixotic theme here. Rambo is on the same side as his government. Both aided the Afghanistan *mujahideen* in their war with the Soviet Union. As such, there is no sense of betrayal or anger against his country for not living up to its ideals. With the larger moral implications stripped from the action, the movie becomes just an action adventure film.

5. See the historical arguments and empirical data in Arrighi (2005a, 2005b), Kennedy (1987), and Bergesen and Sonnett (2001).

6. These international crusades were also combined with periodic acts of national purification throughout the sixteenth century. "Having expelled Jews in 1492, Moors in 1502 and 1525, and having persecuted *marranos* and 'Erasmians' throughout the

sixteenth century, Spain expelled the last pseudo-religious minority, the so-called *Moriscos,* in 1609" (Wallerstein 1974:194).

7. For a review of the evidence, see Chase-Dunn (1998).

8. For an early effort at linking patterns of style in the fine arts with cycles of hegemony and rivalry in the world-system, see Bergesen (1996).

9. Within the sociology of culture there are a variety of perspectives and debates over the relationship of social structure and cultural objects. Are they mere reflections, as in the classic Durkheimian notion of a "collective representation," or do they in some way constitute the social themselves, in the postmodern sense of the discursive formation, or of symbolic power, or as embodiments of cultural reproduction of power and hierarchy? At this point my main purpose is to draw attention at the most general empirical level between an identifiable state of the world-system—the beginning decline of a then-dominant, or hegemonic, power—and the appearance and international popularity of cultural objects with certain themes, such as those discussed earlier in *Don Quixote* and *Rambo.*

CHAPTER FOUR

A Sociology of Monsters

Making Mythical Creatures in the United States and Japan

Walk into any toy store, and the once-predominant American comic book superheroes have been demoted to the back of the store. Whether as action figures, trading cards, video games, or coloring or picture books, Superman, Batman and Robin, Wonder Woman, Spiderman—and even Donald Duck, Mickey Mouse, and Woody Woodpecker—now take a back seat to another set of mythical characters. In store windows, where the most popular and best-selling items are displayed, one finds the Pokemon characters Pikachu, Charizard, Mew, and MewTwo, along with Dragon Ball Z action figures, Transformer robots, and Gundam Wing Mobile Suit humanoid robotic fighter planes.[1]

Popular culture, almost by definition, is constantly changing, and from that point of view, nothing is new. But upon closer examination these characters are fundamentally different from traditional American action heroes. For one thing they look different, from the large eyes of anime characters to the gigantism of the Gundam Wing and Transformer robots. Second, they originate, by and large, from Japan. If world popular culture was once dominated by American images, there has been a noticeable shift East in the origination point of the mythical characters of the most popular of popular culture. Some of this is just differences between nations. With an earlier shift from the global economic predominance of Britain in the nineteenth century to the United States in the twentieth, one would expect different national cultural traditions to also rise and fall. What is interesting now, though, is that the rising zone within the larger world economy is from a different civilizational tradition. With the twenty-first-century rise of East Asian global influence, we see not only an increase in the global consumption of their material goods but their popular cultural imagery as well.

In illustrating these differences between the cultural construction of monsters and mythical creatures in Western and Eastern civilizations, I rely primarily upon objects of popular culture from Japan and the United States. This will be followed by a discussion of two models composed of different cultural algorithms that produce mythical beings that differ in fundamental ways. One is the Mixing Model, and the other is the Essentially Other Model. Finally, I will situate these different kinds of monsters within different types of political systems, and advance some Durkheimian sociology of culture hypotheses linking political context to type of monster. I begin with a comparison of two iconic images from an Asian (Japanese) and a Western (American) cultural tradition: Godzilla and King Kong.

Godzilla and King Kong

Godzilla is a particularly interesting case for it was inspired by, if not directly modeled after, two American movies that appeared just before it came out in 1954. *King Kong* was rereleased in 1952, and in 1953 appeared *The Beast from 20,000 Fathoms*. Both American films were very popular in Japan. The premise of *The Beast* was that atomic bomb tests in the Arctic unleashed a gigantic dinosaur that had been dormant in the ice for millions of years and now, contaminated by radiation, heads to its old breeding ground—today's New York City—leaving a path of death and destruction. This was a direct inspiration for the Japanese film company Toho to develop a similar film (Lees and Cerasini 1998:12). Initially called *Kaitei Niman Mairu Kara Kita Dai Kaiju* (*The Big Monster from 20,000 Miles Underneath the Sea*), this unwieldy title was soon replaced by *Gojira* (1954), which combined the Japanese words for gorilla (*gorira*) and whale (*kujira*). With some new sections added it was retitled *Godzilla, King of the Monsters,* and rereleased for worldwide distribution by an American film company.[2]

The Japanese goal was very much that of the American goal: to produce a monster movie. But the cultural cloth from which it was cut was quite different. Guided by a different set of philosophical assumptions, the Japanese would produce a very different kind of monster. The commercial motivation for both American and Japanese films was identical; what differed was the civilizational context within which that economic motive was realized. Although the monsters in all three movies were gigantic, two of them were creatures from the natural world, and the third, with a radioactive particle beam shooting from its mouth, was clearly from another reality. *The Beast from 20,000 Fathoms* was a dinosaur, King Kong a gorilla, and Godzilla a ...? Notice, I don't have a natural category here, for what kind of earthly creature is Godzilla? True, dinosaurs do not exist now, but they once did, and a giant gorilla is still a gorilla—just large. But what is Godzilla? There are no creatures alive today, nor were there in the past, that have radioactive rays, so Godzilla is obviously mythical. But there are no extra-large gorillas or awakened dinosaurs, either, so they are mythical too. Our question, though, is how and why such differences in mythical beings are constructed.

Generally all cultures—East or West—have a set of mythological monsters, just as, in Emile Durkheim's (1965) classic observation, all societies have some form of religion. But not all monsters look alike, and what I want to focus on here are the different logics, or cultural algorithms—that is, constant sets of operating principles that generate mythical beings with common features across long periods of historical time.

We can identify two cultural logics or models. The first, which we will call the Mixing Model, involves the exaggeration or recombination of characteristics from already existing creatures of the natural world, while the second, the Essentially Other Model, constructs purely imaginary beings from hypothetical worlds. At a general sociological level what we are talking about are different models, cultural logics, or monster-making algorithms that generate ontologically different mythical creatures. Each model produces an equally mythical and equally frightening creature. The difference is one of content, not social function. Both sets of monsters are pressed into service for mythology, religion, popular culture, and constructing legitimations for social inequalities and distributions of power.

Creatures produced by the cultural algorithm of the Mixing Model would include things like a giant ape (*King Kong*), giant ants (the movie *Them!*), a giant squid (the book and movie *Twenty Thousand Leagues Under the Sea*), a giant woman (the movie *The Attack of the 50–Foot Woman*), or a giant snake (the movie *Anaconda*). Creatures generated from the Essentially Other Model would be more otherworldly, such as the smog monster Hedorah from the Godzilla movies, giant Transformer robots, and the various pocket and digital monsters in the Pokemon, Digimon, and Monster Rancher video games and television programs.

Both models produce make-believe creatures. The difference lies in how they construct them: are they exaggerations and/or combinations of elements from this world, or are they more imaginary creatures from hypothetical worlds? There are, of course, exceptions to these general rules. There are exaggerated natural creatures in the Godzilla movies, like Mothra, the giant moth, and some purely imaginary creatures in American horror films, like the creature in the movie *Alien* (1979). But as a general tendency I think it is reasonable to conclude that American monsters tend to be produced by a cultural logic that mixes and exaggerates already existing natural creatures, whereas Japanese mythical beings tend to be altogether more hypothetical and extra-natural.

The Mixing Model

To understand the essence of the Western model of making monsters, we can begin with a simple question: Why is a monster so frightening? Without thinking too much about it, it would seem that there is something about monsters that is dangerous or frightening. But this only begs the question, What makes something dangerous, or induces fright? For example, a wolf can be frightening, as can, under some circumstances, a man, but the combination of the two, a "wolfman" or "werewolf," seems more frightening than the portion of fright contributed by either wolf or man. But why? Where do the added degrees of fright come from that are above and beyond the sum of their partial fright components? There are any number of possible explanations, but let me introduce some ideas from Durkheim on the distinctly social origin of ideas of deviance, danger, scariness, and fright.

There is a calm security that arises from a clearly defined and more or less well-ordered social universe. (Anthony Giddens [1990] calls this the sense of *ontological security*.) This derives from the classic sociological notion that individuals inhabit a social world that involves both forms of physical association—social groups—and socially constructed universes of meaning—culture, broadly conceived. This symbolic universe of received knowledge is categorically divided into various taxonomies of things and states of being. Whether we call it our "habitus" (Bourdieu 1984), "sacred canopy" (Berger 1969), "socially constructed reality" (Berger and Luckmann 1966), "definition of the situation" (Mead 1934; Blumer 1969; Mills 1940; Goffman 1959), or system of "primitive classification" (Durkheim and Mauss 1963), it refers to the cultural construction of a universe of types of beings and their psychological dispositions, a universe within which humans meaningfully act and interpret the world. It is within such a symbolic universe that human life is experienced as normal and legitimate, and as such stable and secure.

But when that categorical order changes, when definitions of creatures vary from the norm, when there is a mixing of categories that violates the socially agreed upon definition of the world with things in their place, then a sense of unease, danger, fright, and anomic terror has been hypothesized to arise (Durkheim 1933; Douglas 1970). If, following this reasoning, there appear types of creatures that violate standard categories, they would constitute a breakdown of, or challenge to, the received category system and, as such, generate anomic feelings of danger and fright.

For example, the anthropologist Mary Douglas (1966) takes the simple idea of "dirt" to unveil how a sense of danger is generated by the larger cultural system of cosmological classification. Following her logic provides us with some ideas as to why certain creatures and not others are considered monsters. The core idea goes back to Durkheim (1933), whose argument about the moral status of being a criminal or deviant is applicable to the status of being a monster. He reasoned, "We must not say that an action shocks the common conscience because it is criminal, but rather that it is criminal because it shocks the common conscience" (Durkheim 1933:81), which we can paraphrase as, "We must not say that a creature is out of place because it is a monster, but rather that it is a monster because it is out of place." So, for instance, possessing exaggerated size is one way of being out of place, but we would not say a creature is gigantic because it is a monster, but rather that it is a monster because it is gigantic. Douglas then generalizes this idea, arguing that "we are left with the very old definition of dirt as matter out of place. Dirt then, is never a unique, isolated event. Where there is dirt there is a system. Dirt is the by-product of a systemic ordering and classification of matter in so far as ordering involves rejecting inappropriate elements" (Douglas 1966:48). As Douglas generalized from Durkheim to dirt, we can generalize from dirt to monsters, arguing that they too are never unique isolated creatures.

Where there are monsters, then, there is a system, as mythical monsters are the by-product of a systematic ordering and classification of creatures, where ordering involves, of necessity, rejecting inappropriate elements. The key idea is the "inappropriate element." When some properties of natural creatures (teeth, legs, head, overall size, and so forth) do not fit the cosmological category to which they belong, they are out of place, and as such they become the source of the anomic terror we recognize as being frightening and dangerous. Douglas uses this logic for an explanation of the abhorrent status of creatures in the biblical admonitions of Leviticus.

> The underlying principle ... in animals is that they shall conform fully to their clan. Those species are unclean which are imperfect members of their class, or whose class itself confounds the general scheme of the world.... In the firmament two-legged fowls fly with wings. On the earth four-legged animals hop, jump or fly. Any class of creatures which is not equipped for the right kind of locomotion in its element is contrary to holiness.... Anything in the water which has not fins and scales is unclean (xi, 10–12).... Four-footed creatures which fly (xi, 20–26) are unclean. Any creature which has two legs and two hands and which goes on all fours like a quadruped is unclean. (Douglas 1966: 69)

If we substitute "monstrous" for "unclean" we have an explanation for our abhorrence of creatures that contravene their categorical type. For example, it isn't a furry coat, claws, and elongated teeth per se that make something a monster, for on a wolf that is its normal classificatory place. But on a man, such teeth, claws, and fur contravene the classification of both man and wolf, and the resultant

"Wolfman" is neither wolf nor man. In violating both categories, a classificatory anomaly is created, and hence it is considered frightening and dangerous.

What is and isn't a monster, then, depends upon a system of natural creature classification and its contravention. A cultural logic, which produces category-contravening creatures, is an algorithm for the production of monsters. This is the central cultural mechanism employed in the West for the social creation of monsters and mythical beings. This algorithm has created mythical beings from the ancient Egyptian figure Anubis, who had the body of a man and the head of a jackal, through the characters of classic Greek mythology, including Achelous, a river god who in confrontation with Hercules, assumed the form of a man with the head of a bull; or Cerberus, a gigantic dog with three heads, a serpentine tail, and a mane of snakes. It also produced the Chimera, with the head and front of a lion, hindquarters of a dragon, and body of a goat; the Echidna, which had the head and upper body of a beautiful woman, while below her waist she was a serpent; and the mythical Harpy, who is half vulture and half woman. The Mixing Model appears to be civilizational in its historical breadth, as it continues into modern times. The algorithm is employed in a number of nineteenth-century novels, including Mary Shelley's *Frankenstein* (1816), John Polidovi's *The Vampyre* (1816), Robert Louis Stevenson's *Dr. Jekyll and Mr. Hyde* (1886), and Bram Stoker's *Dracula* (1897). It is employed in the twentieth and twenty-first centuries as well, with cinematic versions of these novels, plus new mixings, such as the movie *The Fly!* (1958), wherein a scientist's device for transmitting matter goes awry after a fly accidentally enters the chamber, making the scientist emerge with the body of a human and the head and claws of that insect.

Mixing, though, is not limited to body types; it includes personality traits as well. Sometimes the mix involves both mind and body, as in the case of the werewolf, where both the wolf's ferocious nature and patches of fur and elongated teeth are taken on by the human. Similarly, vampires have both the teeth and motives of bats, empowering humans to suck blood from human arteries as bats would from cattle. Various degrees of uncertainty and anomic terror, then, are created when one species takes on the needs, motives, or personality traits of others. But this is not limited to humans taking on animal traits. An inverse mixing also occurs, and it generates fright as well. It is just as frightening when animals assume human motivations. Think of King Kong. The great ape fell in love with a human (obviously a species violation) and showed a degree of human self-consciousness, as when examining his blood-stained fingers after being shot at by airplanes while atop the Empire State Building. Also, like a human lover, it was said he died of a broken heart. "Well, there you have it. Beauty killed the beast"—the famous last line of the original movie.

Another tactic is to impute human personality traits such as revenge and rationality to animals.[3] When they turn on humans, whether as Moby Dick, Orca, or Hitchcock's birds, they are particularly frightening. Human personality traits can also bleed into machines, like the supercomputer "Hal" in Stanley Kubrick's 2001: *A Space Odyssey* (1968), which is eerily human, devious, and frightening, or in a more humorous fashion into the R2D2 and C3PO robots from the *Star Wars* movies.

Mixing has also been extended to combining the human and the mechanical, as in the lead characters in the movie *Robocop* (1987) and the television series *The Six Million Dollar Man* (1972) and *The Bionic Woman* (1976), all of whom had their physical faculties rebuilt with mechanical and electronic devices. The "Terminator" (1984, 1991) characters in the Arnold Schwarzenegger movies were also a terrorizing mix of machine and man.

In principle, then, there is no limit to what can be mixed, for the terror arises from the process of the mixing, not from the content that is mixed. The act of mixing is of such interest that one of the most notorious Western monster stories centers on the mixing process itself, when Dr. Frankenstein assembles his monster. The phenomenon of category blurring remains of great interest and has appeared as a topic of serious academic discourse about the meaning of half-machine/half-human cyborgs (see Haraway 1991).

Along with mixing minds and bodies, category violation can be accomplished through size exaggeration, when, for instance, a normal-sized natural animal (an ordinary great ape) has its size dramatically increased (King Kong). This produces a domino effect, as the oversized creature no longer fits into a normal-sized world, which creates even more crises for normal conceptions of reality. Kong—gigantic, but otherwise a normal great ape—wreaks havoc in New York City, as do the giant ants in *Them!* Being giant ants, they are in no need of hypothetical capabilities, like Godzilla's death ray, to bring havoc to

Los Angeles, just as Jules Verne's giant squid—again, except for the size exaggeration, just a squid—terrorizes Captain Nemo's submarine. Size exaggeration can also go in the other direction. There is terror in the movies *The Incredible Shrinking Man* (1957) and humor in *Honey I Shrunk the Kids* (1989).

Mixing, then, is almost a preoccupation of the Western mind, which seems fascinated by the process and tries endless combinations not only of monsters, but for humor as well. In *The Incredible Mr. Limpet* (1964), Don Knotts's character becomes a fish; in *All of Me* (1984) a woman's soul enters Steve Martin's body; and in *Big* (1988) with Tom Hanks, a young boy's soul is put into an older boy's body. Mix, mix, and mix again: the result is sometimes frightening, sometimes humorous, and sometimes tragic. It can reach exaggerated heights. The comic book character "Jigsaw" has a mechanical right arm, a hairy wolfman-like left arm, a human torso and legs, and a head that is half mechanical and half human. It is mixing in the extreme, where each body part seems to come from someone or something else.

Examples of different kinds of blendings are shown in Figure 4.1. Starting from the right-hand side, the first figure is "Hammerhead," a character from the *Star Wars* movies. Here we have a human body with very elongated arms, gigantic hands, and feet that seem to be those of elephants or some other type of creature. Most dramatically, its head is shaped like that of a hammerhead shark. In the middle is "Bib Fortuna," another *Star Wars* character. He seems to be mostly a normal human being, except for twin growths or tails that come out of the back of his head and are long enough to wrap around his torso. Here we see size distortion plus a transplanted part—whether an animal tail or an elephant's trunk isn't clear. Finally, to the far left is Spiderman. He is a human, Peter Parker by name, who having been bitten by a radioactive spider now possesses many of the attributes of spiders. It is a simple enough mix: spider + man = "Spiderman."

The Essentially Other Model

Whereas the mixing algorithm seems to predominate in the West, it is found less often in Asia, where monsters are less mixtures of natural creatures and more just themselves. In the West monstrousness arises when something goes wrong with a natural being, whether animal,

Figure 4.1. Three examples of mythical creatures created by mixing various aspects of natural reality

human, or machine, but in Asian mythology things do not have to go wrong to create monsters. They simply are who they are. Godzilla isn't a dinosaur who went wrong, he is just himself, Godzilla, for it is his essential being that creates terror. He doesn't have to go wrong—he is wrong already. He is a problem just being himself; no mixture is necessary to create fright and terror.

In this model there is less category mixing. Behind this observation lies a more general sociological point: the stronger the boundaries that make up a classificatory system for types of beings, the less the chance of mixing and contravention. Danger, then, doesn't just come from weak categorical walls that allow a mixing of attributes from different creatures. Creatures that lie outside the system's categories altogether can also create it. Here monsters tend to be less a mixture of a cosmology's categorical infrastructure and more a visitation by creatures outside normal categorical reality. Monsters now come from other worlds. They are not creatures of this world that have gone awry, but visitations from other worlds. Sociological theory stipulates that strong categorical boundaries make things outside their ordered universe particularly dangerous and frightening and, as such, the source of anomic terror.

King Kong is frightening because he is a member of a natural class of creatures that has had its boundaries violated in at least two ways: he is gigantic, and he seems to possess human romantic feelings to the extent of falling in love with a human and purportedly dying of a broken heart. Those category violations create a great fear but also fascination, such that the original 1933 movie has been remade a number of times (most recently in 2005). Now consider Godzilla. He is not an exaggeration of any known creature on earth, past or present. He is large, but his monstrousness doesn't arise from size exaggeration per se. He is not just a large dinosaur, an escapee from *Jurassic Park* (1993), a movie about dinosaurs being alive today that had been cloned from the DNA found within insects preserved in pieces of amber. Godzilla's size contributes to his frightening presence, but the key point is that he is neither a size-exaggerated natural being nor the product of any mixing process; his frightening nature does not arise from mixing what appears to be a *Tyrannosaurus rex* body with, say, Stegosaurus plates running down his spine (see Figure 4.2). Godzilla is a completely self-contained package, not a mix of other creatures. Giant ants are frightening, but they are still ants; a giant

74

Figure 4.2. Godzilla: Example of the Essentially Other Model of making monsters

squid is threatening, but still nothing but a squid; a gigantic ape is terrifying, but only a few evolutionary notches away from humanity. But Godzilla isn't a giant anything. He naturally exists in that size. He is not a distortion of any past or present natural creature.

Second, Godzilla's otherworldliness can also be seen in the absence of many of the human motives that animated King Kong, who was captured, tied down, taken from his home, and put on humiliating display. Kong's reaction was understandable rage, but Godzilla, other than being awakened, had no understandable reason for destroying Tokyo. The Japanese did not go out to capture him, tie him up, transport him to Tokyo, or put him on display. Furthermore, he was awakened by the Americans and their nuclear testing, not by the Japanese. He doesn't, however, wade into San Francisco Bay for rightful revenge, but instead heads for Tokyo Bay. But why Japan? What did the Japanese ever do to him?

Godzilla, then, seems much more supernatural, an almost abstract power or presence that periodically intrudes into the affairs of ordinary people without warning or probable cause. King Kong, in contrast, is much more natural and understandable in his response to what had been done to him. From this perspective Godzilla seems to have little of what we understand as "personality." He is mostly an uncontrollable force from somewhere that has descended without warning upon the Japanese. Both Kong and Godzilla are, of course, just creations of the human imagination, but it seems that the creation process employs different cultural algorithms. The interesting question is, Why do different civilizations seem to prefer different models of monster making?

Civilizational Algorithms

Perhaps what we mean by civilization is a cultural constant that can be represented by such algorithms as these. Because of the great width of geographical space and long periods of historical time required to call something civilizational, what is required is a core set of repetitive dynamics, rules, models, or algorithms that yield a cultural outcome with some kernel of constancy: dragons, Godzilla, and Transformer robots on one side, and satyrs, werewolves, and Robocops on the other. The specifics of monsters seem more like placeholders, while the logic of their essential character seems a constant—hence the civilizational reference.

This point certainly seems to hold for the traditions of monster making we have reviewed here. These traditions, East or West, show a great deal of historical continuity. The propensity to make mythical beings by mixing is a constant feature of the Western imagination since at least the time of classical Greek mythology, if not earlier. What gets mixed varies over time, of course. Early on it was primarily a mixture of animals, or animals and humans (centaur, satyr, minotaur, werewolf); in later years it came to include humans and supernatural powers (Superman, Wonder Woman, the X-Men, Spiderman, and so forth); then humans and machinery (Robocop, Hal); and finally humans and virtual reality (*The Matrix*). Similarly, in Asia, from the ancient dragon down through Godzilla to the digital monsters of television, video games, and action figures, the propensity of the East Asian imagination tends toward more powerful otherworldly creatures. As with the West, the Eastern cultural logic appears to be highly constant, with change limited to subject matter or ? placeholders that reflect the contingencies of technological advancement and historical change. Their otherworldliness, though, is held constant.

Early on it was the dragon. Powerful and otherworldly, it was a mysterious force capable of good and evil that penetrated the daily lives of ordinary people. The dragon can be seen as a historically contingent placeholder that was later filled by a figure such as Godzilla, as noted here:

> Yet Godzilla keeps rising again and again, long past the time when nuclear test bans and the end of the Cold War have rendered his original message irrelevant. That's because Godzilla was more than a message to begin with. He's supposed to be a dinosaur ... but the fishermen of Odo Island identify him with a legendary monster of the past that could be appeased only by virgin sacrifices—which puts him squarely in the tradition of the fire-breathing dragons of folklore. (Pierce 1998:17)

The ancient dragon is believed "to roam beneath the surface of the earth, and woe unto him who digs into the ground at the wrong time of the year and injures so much as a single scale of this mysterious mythical creature" (Morgan 1942:7). Godzilla similarly slept beneath the ground until awakened by the testing of atomic weapons. Later, in *King Kong vs. Godzilla* (1963), it is an American nuclear submarine that unknowingly released Godzilla when it exploded an iceberg. In *Godzilla vs. the Sea Monster* (1966/1969), it is a bolt of lightning that awakens Godzilla within underground caverns, and in *Son of Godzilla* (1967/1968) various weather experiments on Zorgel Island create extremely high temperatures, which hatch an infant Godzilla.

Dragon and Godzilla are also both reptilian, with powerful fiery breaths, who carry out good and evil deeds. There is "the 'evil' Godzilla, who devastates Tokyo ... as well as the 'good' Godzilla, who defends humanity against other monsters" (Pierce 1998:17). There are any number of social issues that are addressed with Godzilla as a metaphoric tool. In *Godzilla vs. Hedorah* (the smog monster), what is being represented is environmental pollution; in *Mothra vs. Godzilla* a stand is taken on government corruption and the excesses of capitalism; in *The Return of Godzilla* the issue again is nuclear testing; and in *Godzilla vs. King Ghidorah* the issue is Japan's position in the world economy. As the following quote suggests, Godzilla is almost an algorithm, that is, an empty metaphor that can be filled with the issues of the day.

> Given the host of weapons used against him, it is evident that Godzilla has infinite powers of regeneration. But that regeneration can also be considered a metaphor: Godzilla lives on and on because he can always be reborn in whatever guise works best for the time, and can be invested with whatever greater significance suits our psychological needs. (Pierce 1998:17)

There seems to be a cultural algorithm here for the construction of monsters with degrees of freedom allowed so that historical contingency can insert relevant images appropriate to the times. The same cultural logic that produced the dragon, given the more recent concern with nuclear war, radioactivity, and the discovery of dinosaurs, takes this new input data and produces a figure like Godzilla—or, given the development of robotics, outputs gigantic robots, as seen in Transformers and Gundam Wing comic books, action figures, and TV series.

The monster-making algorithm is constrained differently in these two models, so that, in principle, given the same thematic input, each model outputs different kinds of mythical creatures. The algorithm of the Essentially Other Model takes historically contingent symbols, imagery, and ideas and produces mythical beings that are (1) otherworldly in origin in terms of both their physical looks and personality, (2) singularly themselves in essence (not mixtures), (3) quite powerful, and (4) virtually unrestrained by human or natural processes. The Mixing Model also takes historical realities as inputs, but is constrained to yield mythical creatures that (1) exist or existed in the natural world; (2) have some aspect of their physical appearance modified, usually in terms of size exaggeration, or being physically or psychologically mixed with other living creatures, machines, or virtual realities; and (3) are less powerful and as such often subjugated to human control. Sometimes the surface appearance of monsters suggests they were produced by the same underlying logic. With reptilian body and horse-like head, the dragon seems like a product of the Western Mixing Model, in this case, say, horse and lizard. But the essence of the dragon is not a lizard that runs like a horse, or a horse with the poisonous bite of a lizard. The dragon's essence is singular, not composite, and though the parts are from different creatures, that is understood as the very nature of dragons.

To separate the algorithmic logic of these models from their thematic input we can look for different outputs given similar historical input. For instance, given the input of the mid-twentieth-century nuclear age and radioactivity, the Mixing Model produces size exaggeration, like the radioactive ants in the movie *Them!*, or the young man bitten by a radioactive spider to create Spiderman. The Essentially Other Model took the same inputs and produced the nonnatural and the uniquely itself (nonmixed) creature we know as Godzilla. For both algorithms the same historical input: the atomic age. And from each a different cultural output: mixed natural versus extra-natural beings.

Consider another example of the same input yielding divergent outputs. The emergence of robotics provides a more neutral case of a worldwide technological innovation that is transformed differently by the two models. With robotics as input, the algorithmic constraints of the Mixing Model produce robotic figures that are a mix of machinery and human personality traits, such as R2D2 ("Artoo") and C3PO from the *Star Wars* movies. Although Artoo looks like a fireplug with no eyes to look at you or mouth to smile at you, he is clearly lovable and endearing, and with his squeaks and squeals shows a child-like impatience to be loved and included. C3PO looks like a human being and also has a very humanlike personality, worrying, complaining, and being grouchy and touchy. These robotic figures are roughly human-sized and partake in human activities. Artoo is a copilot of a starfighter, and C3PO translates languages and scientific manuals.

If R2D2 and C3PO were man-made, acted human, and served humans, consider the origin and interests of the huge Transformer robots of Japanese comics, television, movies, and action figures, the products of the Essentially Other Model:

> Four million years ago they came from *Cybertron,* a world composed entirely of machinery ... a world torn by an age-old war between the heroic *Autobots* and the evil *Decepticons.* These incredibly powerful living robots, capable of converting themselves into land and air vehicles, weapons and other mechanical forms, continue their conflict here on *Earth.* (Quoted from the comic book *The Transformers,* Hasbro-Bradley, Inc., 1984)

Coming from their own mythical planet and operating on nonorganic principles, these robots are neither man-made entities (Artoo/C3PO), evolutionary isolates (King Kong), experimental errors (*The Fly*), or the result of accidental bites (werewolf, Spiderman). They conduct their age-old feuds while being, by and large, indifferent to human concerns. As explained in Hasbro-Bradley comics, the Autobots, losing their battle in space to the evil Decepticons, decide to send their spaceship filled with battling Autobots and Decepticons on a suicide course to crash into Earth. The ship smashes into a volcano and remains embedded for four million years. Nothing disturbs their dormant state until the volcano erupts and uncovers their ship, awakening both the good Autobots and the evil Decepticons, and their battle resumes once again, this time on Earth. Interestingly enough, the dragon and Godzilla are also awakened from beneath the ground. And when Transformer robots fight each other it has the feel of combat above and beyond humans, as if a war between the gods, similar to Godzilla's battles with other monsters. They seem more mythical struggles between forces of good and evil than the rage of a gigantic caged ape (King Kong) or a tyrannosaurus loose in San Diego (*The Lost World: Jurassic Park,* 1997).

Durkheim and Monsters

There appear to be differences in types of monsters. Is there any plausible sociology concerning properties of the sociopolitical systems in which they are produced that might offer some working hypotheses as to their origin? Consider for a moment the logic classically used by Durkheim when he linked the experience of all sorts of powers and forces with the types of societies in which they appeared. The specifics of the experience of force were somewhat irrelevant, for they were symbolic representations of more fundamental forces and structures of social power.

In that regard, dragons may be hammered out of bronze, Godzilla screened on chemically developed film, and pocket monsters (Pokemon) realized in the virtual reality of video games, but the underlying logic of an otherworldly creature seems constant. Durkheim reasoned that what constituted the specific character of gods did not matter either, for they were collective representations of societal structures of power. In a similar vein, there is something extraordinary about all the mythical beings and monsters considered here. They are not part of the natural world, even if the parts of some of them start out that way in the Mixing Model. Durkheim reasoned that the only thing that could inspire individuals to talk of such extraordinary beings was the only extra-individual presence that characterized people's lives: the power of the collective reality of the societies in which they were embedded. The social, especially as institutionalized power, was a thing in itself that humans symbolically represented with a variety of images that had varying degrees of power themselves.

The kinds of monsters we have been considering could be considered in the same way. This insight is further specified with the observation that as the power of the state grows, so does the imagined power of that society's mythical monsters. It is sociologically understandable, then, that China, with its political tradition of powerful emperors and imperial courts, would produce a cultural tradition of powerful mythical creatures like the dragon. The Durkheimian point is that the presence of imperial political systems provides the concentration of power that, over time, comes to be collectively expressed as images of mythical figures with a similar potency.

> The Dragon is said to be the emblem of guardianship and vigilance.... The throne of the Empire became the Dragon throne. The ... coat-of-arms

from the Han to the Ch'ing dynasty consisted of a pair of dragons fighting for a pearl [and] the robes of the Emperor, as well as many articles of his household, all bore the design of the five-clawed dragon. This five-clawed creature was the emblem of Imperial authority, while the lesser officials used the four-clawed Dragon. (Morgan 1942:7)

There are, of course, dragons in the mythology of the West, but they seem less powerful and more open to control by humans. This is dramatically seen in the myth of St. George and the Dragon wherein the dragon is slain. A similar reduction in dragon power can be seen in movies like *Pete's Dragon* (1977), where a kid befriends a klutzy dragon, and in *Dragonheart* (1996), a buddy movie about a dragon and a medieval knight working a protection racket on the local peasantry. Western dragons also seem more lovable, as in the Peter, Paul, and Mary song *Puff, the Magic Dragon,* with its soft, friendly, cuddly lyrics:

Puff, the magic dragon, lived by the sea
And frolicked in the autumn mist in a land called Honalee.
Little Jackie Paper loved that rascal Puff
And brought him strings and sealing wax and other fancy stuff.

Following this reasoning, it could be hypothesized that a society with a strong and powerful state should produce strong and powerful mythical beings. Also, if the state is the structural representation of the collectivity, then in its purest and most unalloyed form it should be culturally represented as the purest and most unalloyed of essentially other mythical beings. If, in contrast, the state's power is compromised by being mixed in with the interests, goals, and purposes of society's constituent groups and individuals, then that essential otherness of a monster should be replaced by mythical beings who themselves are constituted from mixtures of natural creatures.[4] If recurrent images of monsters are tied to the structure of political power, then not only will the more powerful state yield more powerful images (monsters), but the more distant that state apparatus is from the control of civil society, the more distant will the origin of those monster images seem from everyday reality.

Following this theoretical logic, might it be plausible that ancient China, with its political system of all-powerful emperor and imperial court, with a wide gap between itself and the mass of the peasantry, constitutes the power substrate that over the centuries comes to be represented in that system's cultural imagery as that very distant and powerful creature the dragon? And isn't it also sociologically possible that in ancient Greece, with its system of compromised state power (rudimentary democratic structures of the *polis*), where the interests of individuals and civil society are regularly mixed in with those of the city-state, over time there would arise a mythology tilted toward mythical beings as mixes of natural creatures and/or supernatural forces?

Turning to more recent times, what could be inferred about the political system in which a figure like the comic book character "Jigsaw" would appear? Remember, he is a mix of elements: his right arm is mechanical, his left is that of some beast, his legs and torso are human, and his face is half mechanical. Following the propositions just explicated, one could conclude that such a collective representation should appear in a very plural society with a high degree of social mixing and complex checks and balances on political power. "Jigsaw" is an American comic book character, and the structure of that symbol fits, to some degree, the plural power structure of the United States. Might it also be a reasonable working hypothesis that in Japan—where "the half-century rule by a single party has stunted the growth of Japanese democracy, experts say, and its effects are still being felt today" (Onishi 2005:A4)—you might also find the emergence on the symbolic plane of a single all-powerful mythical being, like Godzilla? This is not to say that Godzilla is a one-to-one mirror image of the Japanese political system, or a collective representation of the Liberal Democratic Party, which was formed in 1955. But it is to suggest that in a cultural tradition where "civil society remains weak [and] those delving into delicate issues, like human rights, freedom of information and the workings of government, wield little influence" (Onishi, 2005:A4), is a sociopolitical context in which essentially other, as opposed to mixing, imaginary creatures might be more welcomed.

More generally, the theoretical argument laid out here suggests a continuum of both political systems and types of monsters. At one end are systems where there is little or no sharing, or mixing, of power. These types of systems would produce imaginary creatures that are more powerful and morphologically more the singular essential entity. In effect, pure, unalloyed state power produces pure, unalloyed monsters. At the other end of the continuum, political power is more shared and compromised by the interests of individuals and civil society. Here we find monsters and other mythical creatures that have their being penetrated by the bodily morphology and/or psychology of other creatures. In principle there is also a one-to-one logic with these hypotheses. Increase state power a unit, raise monster strength a unit; widen the gap between rulers and ruled a unit, widen the distance of origin for monsters a unit; raise the sharing of power a unit, raise creature mixing a unit. In principle, an idealized polity of perfect democracy would have a mythology where its monsters were perfectly mixed creatures, and an idealized autocracy of totally unshared power would have pure monsters of a very otherworldly origin. While there are no such idealized polities, this theoretical idea helps make sense of why it was that a democratic ancient Greece would give birth to a complex mythology of so many mixed natural creatures, and why ancient China, with an imperial hierarchy at the top of which sat an all-powerful emperor, would produce the image of the unique being that is the all-powerful dragon. Two different political traditions, two different mythological traditions. A single unrestrained actor as the embodiment of the state yields a single all-powerful monster. Mixing individuals and groups within the state yields mixed creatures as the monsters of that mythology.

Conclusion

Let me conclude with a cautionary note. While East and West seem the historical origin of these two different models of monster making, global social change works toward eroding these differences. The commonality of societal form resulting from globalization diminishes differences, as does the seeming worldwide shift to various forms of democratic political systems. That we can still note different tendencies in the morphology of mythological creatures in this age of globalization is amazing. Perhaps it reflects global cultural lag. At present we simply don't know how long it takes selected features of structured political power to be translated into works of imagination that go on through the symbolic reproduction of ritual to become enduring cultural images. What we do know is that the difference between mixing and otherness as cultural procedures for creating imaginary beings seems to be favored by different civilizational traditions. But will the commonalities produced by globalization eventually blend them, or is there a synthetic model on the horizon reflecting the distinctly global aspect of world culture above and beyond "East" and "West" (let alone other civilizational traditions)? Or, can countries switch back and forth between models? When in an autocratic or imperial phase will imagery drift toward the powerful, distant, and different? And in times characterized by pluralism, compromise, and more active participatory democracy, will the blended and mixed imagery regain its hegemony? These are all questions that future empirical research will have to help us sort out.

Notes

1. New popular cultural figures are constantly emerging, and readers should feel free to plug in their favorites, or, if new ones arise, to see how they may or may not follow the logic explicated here.

2. In 1954 there was another American horror film about nuclear testing, *Them!* Here a constantly reproducing colony of gigantic mutant ants spawned by nuclear testing in the New Mexico desert was breeding and causing havoc in the sewers beneath Los Angeles. Two years later Toho Pictures brought out *Rodan,* a film in which deep excavations in a mine uncovered giant insects that were killing the miners.

3. Interestingly, with growing evidence demonstrating that animals possess a variety of mental capacities, the mechanism of animals with humanlike cognitive capacities may seem less and less frightening as it becomes more and more normalized. This does not invalidate the general theory, for this new evidence is simply changing the underlying category system, making it natural for great apes to use language, dolphins to communicate, parrots to count, and so forth. To create new monsters, what will be necessary is the contravention of this new category system. Since it is the contravention rather than the substance of the creature, this will create terror just as well.

4. Swanson (1967) elaborated the Durkheimian link between social power and the potency of mythological creatures by arguing that if a collectivity exists as a thing in itself, it could act. But to do that it would need some arrangement for making collective decisions and taking collective action. For most societies this takes the form of what we mean by government or the state. Importantly, the state varies in terms of how much it allows the penetration of the interests of its constituent individuals and civil society into this structure for collective decision making. Broadly speaking, electoral politics, multiparty systems, constitutionalism, and representational democracies are the most well-known institutional arrangements for allowing the intrusion of the interests of civil society into the political structure designed to represent the societal corporate interest, the state. At the other end of the continuum, emperors, despots, kings, dictators, and various kinds

of authoritarian and single-party regimes are the best-known historical examples of systems that represent the interests of the state at the expense of those of civil society. At one end of this continuum would be societies in which the interests of subgroups were given a prominent place in making and taking collective action; at the other end would be societies where the interests of the corporate political structure, the state, were given institutional priority over the interests and purposes of society's constituent groups. For a set of empirical indicators for the Swanson conception of societal corporateness, see Bergesen (1984).

CHAPTER FIVE

A Sociology of Toys

How Transformers and Spiderman Embody the Philosophies of East and West

SAILOR MOON IS A CARTOON TELEVISION SERIES about teenage girls that originated in Japan. The heroine is a regular junior high school student who is able to "morph," or somehow instantaneously transform into a girl with supernatural powers to fight a variety of mythical monsters.

When the teenager becomes Sailor Moon, she becomes a kind of crime- or monster-fighting "superhero" similar to Batman or Superman. But she doesn't go to the Batcave and change clothes to drive away in something like a Sailor Moonmobile, nor does she run to the nearest telephone booth to take off her clothes (as does Clark Kent) to reveal that she is really Sailor Moon. Instead, when she wants to turn herself into Sailor Moon, and her friends into Sailor Cadets, she just says, "Everyone! Let's morph!" and in what can only be described as some sort of cosmic transformation, they all change from one state of being into another—that is, they instantly reincarnate from being Bunny and girlfriends to Sailor Moon and Sailor Cadets.

Such morphing from one bodily form to another is not limited to a single program. It appears quite widely in Japanese popular culture. The *Mighty Morphin Power Rangers* is another television program that originated in Japan. The central idea has been recycled in a number of different versions but remains basically the same: a group of teenagers are given the power to "morph" into a fighting force with supernatural abilities, becoming Power Rangers. Like Sailor Moon, they are now ready to fight evil. In one state of existence they are teenagers in the natural world; in a flash of light, they "morph," or somehow instantaneously transform, into Power Rangers dressed in brightly colored suits and helmets with dark visors. Once again, they don't just go into a phone booth and take off their teenage clothes to reveal their brightly colored Power Ranger jumpsuits. The path to becoming a superhero in Japanese popular culture seems fundamentally different from that of their American counterparts.

Such morphing can also be seen in video games, television programs, and trading cards that feature lovable and cute "pocket monsters" (Pokemon). In 1995 Nintendo introduced a Pocket Monsters program for its video game system in Japan. It was very popular, and within two years 151 such Pokemon had been introduced to Japanese children. In 1998 Pokemon came to the United States.

Pokemon seem quite similar to folk Shinto ideas of *kami*:

> The word *kami* refers, in the most general sense, to all divine beings of heaven and earth that appear in the classics. More particularly, the *kami* are ... spirits.... In principle human beings, animals, trees, plants, mountains, oceans—all may be *kami*.... The Japanese people believe in and worship ancestral *kami*, household *kami*, occupational *kami*, the *kami* of local and national communities, food *kami*, plant and animal *kami*, the *kami* of nature—a countless host of *kami*. Fellowship with these *kami* is affected through worship in the form of traditional rituals. (Ichiro et al. 1981:37–40)

Pokemon appear to be just such *kami*-like spirits. "Electrode" and "Eletabuzz" are like spirits of electricity, "Magneton" is like a spirit being of magnetism, "Geodude" is rock-like, "Graveler" is like gravel, and so on. Some are plants and animals, but others are more abstract entities, like "Muk," who looks like oozing slime, and "Grimer," who resembles a mound of grime. There is a spirit representation of coughing named "Koffing," one of wheezing—eponymously named—and even a tangled-hair Pokemon named "Tangela." Because Shinto has been an indigenous Japanese folk tradition for over two thousand years, it doesn't seem that the deeply felt presence of *kami* would suddenly disappear. In the same way that Godzilla can be seen as following in the tradition of the ancient dragon iconography, so too can the multiple spirit beings that are Pokemon be seen as following in the tradition of Shinto *kami*. To paraphrase Carl von Clausewitz on war, the popular culture of Pokemon may very well be the continuation of *kami* by other means.

Similar to Pokemon are "Digimon," or digital monsters, which also are the subject of a cartoon series and video games. After originating in Japan they too went on to appear on American television. These digital monsters also possess the ability to morph, transform, or somehow reincarnate themselves from one form of existence to another. At one moment they are cute and lovable, but they can "digivolve" into other kinds of monsters. In one comic book, a digital monster says to itself, "Tsunomon digivolve to Gabumon" and, instantaneously, in the same cartoon panel, separated only by a lightning-like line, Tsunomon (a floating head with a smiling face) reappears as Gabumon (a creature with claws, one horn, saber-toothed tiger fangs, and clenched fists).

Whether it is humans "morphing" (Sailor Moon, Power Rangers), mechanical robots "transforming" (Transformers), or mini-monsters "digivolving" (Digimon, etc.), these inventions of Japanese popular culture all possess the capacity to instantaneously blink out of one material incarnation and reappear in another. To appreciate the uniqueness of this reality jumping, compare the teenagers in *Sailor Moon* with Batman's fellow crime fighter Robin ("Dick Grayson"), who is also a teen and just as interested in fighting evil. How does Dick Grayson (a former circus performer) change into "Robin" (a superhero crime fighter)? Does he just say "let's morph" and instantly become Robin; or does his senior partner say "Bruce Wayne digivolve into Batman," and does he then, in a blink, in a ripple in time, somehow metamorphically change from billionaire industrialist to Batman? Of course not. Instead, Wayne and Grayson go down to the Batcave beneath their house, change clothes, and get into their Batmobile and drive off. Notice: there is no jumping between body forms required for their civilian to superhero transformation. They remain within one reality. They just change their clothes and get into their car—a special car admittedly, but just a car that they keep in their garage. As noted earlier, however, the Power Ranger teens don't go into a changing room to dress in their helmets and jumpsuits; instead, as normal teens they run and jump through something like a ring of fire, coming out on the other side cosmically reconstituted as powerful beings known as "Power Rangers."

Bruce Wayne and Dick Grayson just change clothes; as does Clark Kent (alias Superman) when he exits the phone booth wearing his trademark blue tights, red trunks, and cape. Do the clothes of Batman or Superman give them any additional powers above what they already have? I don't think so. Certainly not Superman. I have seen him perform feats of strength or use his X-ray vision while still incarnated as Clark Kent. This suggests that he is already both human and superhuman in a single body form. That is, he is a blend or *mix* of human and superhuman essences. He can use his powers as either Superman or as Clark Kent, although, of course, he prefers to use them when dressed as Superman. But when forced to use X-ray vision to see through a wall, or to raise a hand to keep a falling boulder from hurting someone, Clark Kent has that power, for Superman and Clark Kent are one and the same. Therefore, Clark Kent doesn't need to "morph" or "transform" into Superman. He already *is* Superman—and Clark Kent. Not so, though, with the teenagers who populate the Japanese-originated fictive characters of Sailor Moon and the Power Rangers. They may start out as what seem to be Japanese Clark Kents, but they cannot just take off their clothes and become supernatural; that requires an act of reincarnation from one state of being to another.

These differences between Japanese and American popular culture might just be two different ways of imagining fictive characters. The question I would like to raise, though, goes deeper. Why do people in these cultures imagine differently, and more specifically, why does one tradition allow for a mixing of realities and essences in a single body while the other seems to favor jumping from body to body, that is, reincarnating from essence to essence? I propose that it is because these differences in popular culture reflect, or embody, different philosophical or religious assumptions about the nature of reality itself. Within one cultural worldview, superhuman and human capacities are assumed to be able to coexist in a stable condition within a single body; within the other, this isn't considered possible. In this second tradition the philosophical sense of being is morphologically locked into one reality or another. One is either Bunny or Sailor Moon; one isn't Clark Kent and Superman in the same body form.

This is because there are different cultural logics for making hypothetical beings, whether in classic myth or in current popular culture.

If a civilization's cultural category system is composed of more permeable walls, then not only can different attributes of natural creatures seep into each other (e. g., wolf + man = Wolfman; machine + man = Robocop), but natural and supernatural realities seep into each other as well (e. g., woman + supernatural powers = Wonder Woman; man + supernatural powers = Superman). Such cultural predispositions pave the way for the Mixing Model that we encountered in the previous chapter, a civilizational algorithm for blending or mixing essences between different worlds as a procedure for producing fictional creatures. From centaurs in Greek mythology to X-Men in American popular culture, this is a long and consistent civilizational propensity. But not all civilizations have such porous cosmological categories, and as such there is much less seepage of attributes from creature to creature, or from the supernatural to natural in other traditions. This condition gives rise to what I have called the Essentially Other Model, a second civilizational tendency found more frequently in Asian cultures. Here mythological beings, in historic myth (dragons) and contemporary popular culture (Godzilla), tend to be of an altogether different cosmological type than what is found in the normal daily reality of the world. Mixing is downplayed and essential differences are emphasized.

Given the cultural condition of a semipermeable cosmological membrane, a mythical person can be imagined to exist in two realities at the same time, as categorical essences bleed into each other. Because of this cultural condition, a human being and the powers of a supernatural reality can stably reside in a single biological form, as in the fusion that we know as Clark Kent/Superman. Or, the properties of a this-worldly creature, like a spider, can reside in a stable condition within the biological form of a human being, as with Spiderman. Ordinary humans can also suffer mutations, creating the mythical X-Men. Machine and man can coexist as well with no operational problems. Think of Robocop. The bleeding goes both ways: A computer can have a human-like personality. Think of HAL in Stanley Kubrick's film 2001: A Space Odyssey.

This is a very deep Western assumption, characterizing religion as well as myth and popular culture. Within the Christian faith, Jesus is assumed to be both man and Son of God, both human and divine within the same bodily incarnation. This Christian assumption is perhaps the ultimate example of the operation of the Western Mixing

Model, where the divine (one reality) and the here and now (another reality) are combined in a stable bodily existence (Jesus). To see a different approach, compare Jesus of Nazareth with Prince Siddhartha Gautama of India. Both are mortals. One is considered by his followers to be both divine (the Christ) and human (Jesus of Nazareth); the other is considered to have been human (Prince Siddhartha) who after extensive meditation became—or, in the language we have been using here, "morphed" or "transformed" into—a realized being (the Buddha). At that point he was no longer Prince Siddhartha. The Buddha, unlike Jesus, is not considered to be simultaneously man and realized being. He is first one, and then the other. On the religious plane, the words of such cosmic jumping are those of "reincarnation," "realization," or becoming "enlightened." On the plane of popular culture, it is a matter of "morphing," "transforming," or "digivolving." The underlying cultural assumption that makes both possible, though, may be the same.

In cultures with porous cosmological categories, essences of different types of beings and realities have a tendency to mix, and so the idea that Clark Kent could at the same time have the power of Superman is plausible. No transforming, morphing, or digivolving is required in this type of culture; the principals are both ordinary (Clark Kent, Peter Parker) and extraordinary (Superman, Spiderman) at one and the same time. But in another civilization that lacks porous cosmological boundaries, its mythology, popular culture, and religion do not feel comfortable with mixed essences, and so when people imagine they conceptualize beings that are in one state or another. There are, therefore, the people of Japan, and Godzilla, Transformers, Pokemon, Digimon, and so forth. There isn't a Godzilla-man or a Godzilla-woman, or a Tokyo newspaper reporter equivalent to Clark Kent who goes into a phone booth to become Godzilla-man. Nor is there a Bruce Wayne who goes down to his Godzilla Cave, dresses up in his Godzilla outfit, and drives into Tokyo to fight crime in his Godzilla-mobile.

But how then do humans become superheroes in Japan? If an all-powerful essence is not part of their being, how do they acquire it? The answer is they can't, and so what is left is the option to jump over the impenetrable categorical barrier reincarnating from teen, Bunny, to super-powerful entity, Sailor Moon; from teens to Power Rangers; or, within mythical realities themselves, from Tsunomon to Gabumon.

Think about it: Here you have a floating head with a smile (Tsuno-mon) that needs to get stronger. Does he, like Superman, just go into a phone booth and reappear as Gabumon? No, for there is no cosmo-logical mixing of essences and realities in this culture. Tsunomon's only choice is to category jump, leap realities, or reincarnate from one state of being to another. Given a civilization with more porous cosmological categories, one might imagine that a floating-headed and smiling Tsunomon was really, underneath, a creature with claws, saber-toothed fangs, and clenched fists, and all it needed to do was to take off its Tsunomon clothes and reveal its Gabumon nature. But in Japanese popular culture it doesn't work that way.

Bunny doesn't go to a phone booth for a costume change, nor to the Sailor Moon Cave; she just yells "Let's morph!" and jumps over her nonpermeable cosmological membrane to reincarnate as Sailor Moon. From a sociology of knowledge perspective, a categorical grid that is impermeable constitutes a cultural precondition for the emer-gence of philosophical and religious systems that feature reincarna-tion as a central mechanism. This is because there are layers within a cultural system. At a deeper level they constitute conceptions of ultimate reality and its divisions into types of creatures and physical elements—like natural and supernatural realities. Given the precon-dition of a fixed and nonporous category system, a secondary set of beliefs then emerges: reality jumping, or reincarnation, as the only logical mechanism to allow passage from one category of being to another. This is a broad civilizational impulse, ranging from Vedantic thought in India to various Chinese- and Japanese-influenced philoso-phies/religions of East Asia. It exists in high culture philosophy (the theory of incarnation) as well as in low or popular culture (morph-ing, digivolving, transforming). Conversely, a porous set of cultural categories for types of creatures and realities has no need of category jumping, for essences, realities, or properties of different creatures are allowed to blend, mix, and recombine in endless permutations. This principle lies at the heart of Western civilization's assumptions about the malleability of reality, which perhaps makes possible a secondary assumption concerning the perfectibility of humankind that lies at the heart of Western emancipatory social and political ideology.

If you are trapped in one reality, then there is no choice; you must jump, you must reincarnate, and your philosophy must admit the possibility of rips, tears, or blinks in reality to allow this to happen.

Clark Kent benefits from the presence of weak, penetrable boundaries between natural and supernatural realities, allowing extra-normal strength, X-ray vision, and the ability to fly to seep into his being. But no such advantage is awarded to Bruce Lee, Jackie Chan, or any other martial arts hero if they want to fight corruption, crime, and injustice. What abilities and powers can they call upon? Can they take off their clothes to reveal extra-normal powers? No, because strong categorical boundaries prevent such powers from seeping through to animate them. One solution is to "transform" into supernatural crime fighters, like the Power Rangers. But Lee, Chan, and other martial arts heroes don't do this, for theirs is the story of ordinary humans fighting crime and evil. How then do they get their edge? If they don't morph, rely upon pocket monsters, or have Transformer robots as friends, they are stuck in the natural world of their human incarnation, and given this condition they have no choice but to train, discipline, and perfect that bodily incarnation. That is why they become martial arts masters. And that is why Asian, not Western, popular culture produces Kung Fu types of movies.

Whereas Western superheroes get help from a leaky system of cosmological boundaries, nothing has seeped into the strength of Bruce Lee or Jackie Chan. They are only what they make themselves. They have no choice but to be "super" at human abilities—they must become the best at kickboxing, Judo, Kung Fu fighting, and so forth. Clark Kent, of course, doesn't need any of that. He just looks for a phone booth and goes inside to take off his clothes, revealing the Superman self that had been there all along. Superheroes of the American variety, therefore, originate less often in the popular cultural imagination of the Japanese. In Asia, mythical heroes tend to concentrate on one side of the cosmic divide or the other. In extra-ordinary reality, they appear as Godzilla, Transformers, Digimon, Pokemon, and so on. In normal reality, they are Bruce Lee, Jackie Chan, and other martial arts masters. And, of course, there are those who jump between realities: the normal Bunny who reincarnates into Sailor Moon, the normal teens who morph into Power Rangers.

This capacity to engage in the act of jumping from reality to reality, or from body form to body form, is built into the very nature of these characters and toys. Within Eastern civilization's philosophy and religion reside ideas about reincarnation, and within the physical construction of their toys reside physical operations that allow children to change them from one state of material being into another—from, say, a Transformer toy truck into a Transformer toy airplane. Transformers debuted in the United States in 1984 and a few years later were featured in a children's television series, a comic book series, and, in 1995, a movie. In the early 1990s the Transformer idea was reborn with a television series called *Beast Wars,* followed by the series *Beast Machines*; the idea will, no doubt, reappear in other future incarnations. The key point is that these toys are constructed so that their ultimate spirit, soul, or consciousnesses remains constant while their bodily incarnation changes.

If ever there was a toy that captured the Vedantic idea that reality is an illusion (maya), it is Transformers. For instance, the Transformer next to Spiderman in Figure 5.1 is in its "beast" incarnation, but because it comes with swivel joints and hidden machine and body components, it can be bent around by a child and transformed into a "ground assault" vehicle, as seen next to Spiderman in Figure 5.2. Although not shown here, this same toy can be further bent and twisted (transformed) to reincarnate as an airplane or a robot. Importantly, when it reincarnates from beast to vehicle to airplane to robot, its Transformer consciousness (it is the same toy) remains constant while its body form changes. It is like toy maya, or the illusions of Transformer reality. Trucks, beasts, airplanes, and robots come and go, but something like a transcendent Transformer consciousness remains a constant across worldly forms of phenomenal being.

Imagine this Transformer and Spiderman standing together as in Figure 5.1 when they hear that a crime has occurred across town. Let's further assume they both want to go and apprehend the criminals. What will they do? Better, what can they do? The Transformer can transform out of its "beast" incarnation into its "ground assault" vehicle incarnation and drive itself across town (see Figure 5.2). And Spiderman? He can spray his spiderwebs onto buildings and swing across town. But this doesn't involve any transforming, for that ability is already part and parcel of his half-spider, half-human Peter Parker essence. He doesn't transform into Spiderman. He *is* Spiderman; he just puts on a spider outfit to look the part. What is telling is that this particular Spiderman action figure came with a three-wheel motorcycle. But why? One possibility is that because he cannot transform into a vehicle, he has no other way to get across town. Not capable of becoming a motor vehicle, he must ride one instead. Responding

Figure 5.1. "Beast" Transformer toy (left); Spiderman action figure toy (right)

Figure 5.2. "Beast" Transformer toy transformed into "Ground Assault" Transformer toy (left); Spiderman action figure toy riding a three-wheel motorcycle (right)

to our hypothetical crime, Figure 5.2 shows both Transformer and Spiderman moving across town, one on a vehicle, one *as* a vehicle. But, again, why the differences?

Let me suggest it is because Western civilization's deep cosmic assumptions will not allow Spiderman to reincarnate as an assault vehicle, forcing him to find a ride. Alternatively, Eastern civilization's deep assumptions won't allow half-beast and half-vehicle essences to seep into each other, creating the chaotic jumble of Transformer parts seen in Figure 5.3. If the cosmic transformation from beast to vehicle illustrated the reincarnation power of Eastern philosophy (the Transformers change form from Figure 5.1 to Figure 5.2) and the inability of Spiderman to transform, Figure 5.3 shows the opposite effect, a combination of the reality mixing assumption of Western philosophy with an Eastern toy. Here we see Spiderman and the Transformer as half-and-half incarnations. But note their differences. Half-and-half (spider + man = Spiderman) works for the Western toy, but not for the Eastern one, where beast + assault vehicle = chaos, as seen in the jumble of parts in Figure 5.3.

Western philosophical assumptions combined with Eastern toys creates nonsense and nonrecognizable incarnations, as seen in Figure 5.4, which depicts a Transformer toy halfway between its incarnation as a Volkswagen automobile and as a robot, and "Pikachu," halfway between its Pokemon Ball incarnation and its full phenomenal manifestation. It would seem that these toys are to be played with in only one incarnation or another, as shown in Figure 5.5, where we see just the Pokemon Ball. No Pikachu. To philosophically jump realities from ball to pocket monster, the child unzips the cloth ball, folds it inside out, and then re-zips it, yielding the full-blown Pikachu (see Figure 5.6). There is no meaningful halfway state of being for this toy, and when one is forcefully created, as on the left-hand side of Figure 5.4, it is like the jumble of car parts next to it—no coherent essence at all.

When a child twists and turns the parts of a "beast" Transformer, thereby reincarnating it into a "ground assault" Transformer, I don't think it is unwarranted to suggest that this is also, at the level of implicit secondary socialization, the symbolic reproduction of underlying religious and philosophical outlooks. This is because the move from beast to motor vehicle is an enactment of the reincarnation process, where the Transformer's consciousness is held constant while its maya-like plastic toy forms are clearly transitory.

Figure 5.3. Transformer Toy as half "beast" and half "ground assault vehicle" (left); Spiderman as half spider essence and half human being (right)

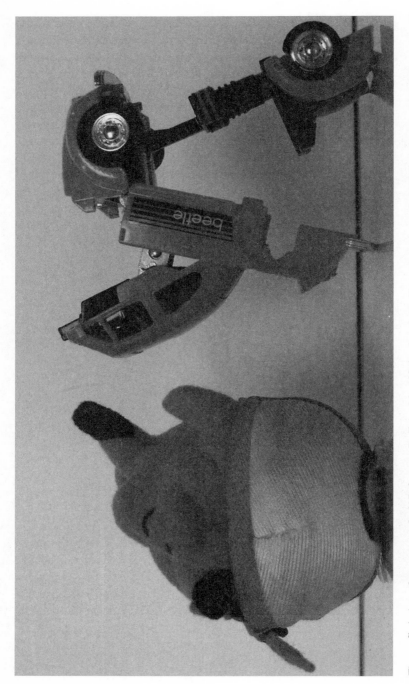

Figure 5.4. A pocket monster half Pokemon Ball and half Pikachu (left); Transformer toy, half Volkswagen automobile and half robot (right)

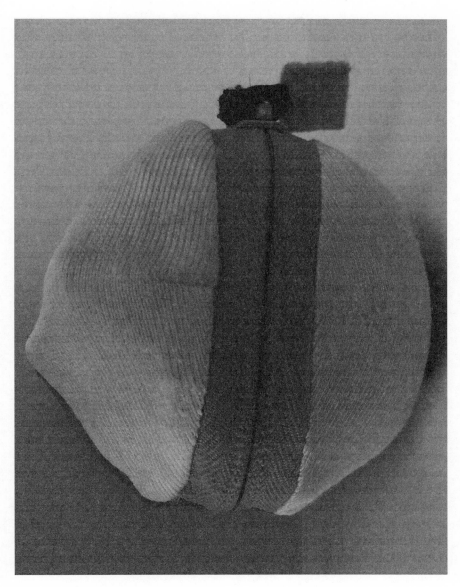

Figure 5.5. A Pokemon Ball

Figure 5.6. Pikachu

Further, with each new incarnation the Transformer's consciousness is increasingly experienced as universal and eternal. Body form after body form come and go, which raises the philosophical question of the ultimate reality of this toy. Is the airplane Transformer real? Is the robot Transformer real? Or are the beast and ground-assault-vehicle Transformers real? In fact, none of them are real, for they clearly come and go. They are but transitory realities, while something like transcendent Transformer reality, for lack of a better term, is the real, and, in the short time of children's play, the eternally real.

This is also the philosophy of the eternal wheel of life: life, death, and rebirth, everything changing yet everything remaining the same. Beast, robot, airplane, and vehicle: all forms of life, yet all transitory. The act of transforming the toy is not just an illustration of the philosophy of reincarnation, or of the illusion of reality, but also a dramatization of the essential oneness of eternity. Regardless of the number of times a Transformer is transformed, Transformer-being persists, independent of the incarnate forms it takes. Transformer consciousness can live in one incarnation (beast), then die (transform) and become reborn (as an assault vehicle), then die again (transform) and be reborn again (as an airplane), then die again (transform), and once again be reborn (as a robot), and so on. In principle a Transformer toy can transform (reincarnate) for eternity.

Playing with Wonder Woman or Spiderman toys also reaffirms the philosophical assumption that different states of being can reside in a singular body. American-originated toys, brought forth within the principles of Western civilization, are not, however, capable of transformations. They can be action figures. They can have swivel joints, and the child can bend, twist, and fold them, just like Transformer toys. But they can only perform behaviors within their human incarnation. The legs, arms, head, and waist of a GI Joe action figure can be bent and twisted like a Transformer toy, but they are constrained to perform only human or soldier activities. GI Joe is constitutionally incapable of reincarnating into an assault vehicle. This is not just because Transformers have great power. Superman and Spiderman have great power, but they cannot be transformed into cars, beasts, airplanes, or assault vehicles. Reincarnation is simply not part of America's religious tradition, and neither is a transforming American superhero.

Philosophy is, of course, deep and profound, whereas toys are shallow and light. They are designed for children to play with. But even the most shallow forms of popular culture can embody the deepest of philosophical principles. Toys are not, of course, complete expositions of philosophical systems. They may be barely a hint. But they do hint at noticeable philosophical differences, and in examining how toys are put together, and the behaviors they are capable of performing, we can uncover deep assumptions about a culture's view of the ultimate nature of reality.

CHAPTER SIX

Bringing the Art Object Back In

Toward a New Realism in the Sociology of Culture

I WANT TO CONCLUDE WITH A GENERAL theoretical point. The analysis in this book focuses on the specific shape, form, and content of objects of popular culture and art. This has not been a study of how any random piece of popular culture can be defined this way or that, but instead the book has taken great pains to identify specific parts of each object that have contributed to the interpretation it yielded. Such an approach may seem obvious, but this isn't the case, for the reigning theoretical paradigm in the sociology of culture is to focus on how art objects are defined or labeled from the outside rather than on their specific inside shape or form. As a result, the art object is no longer seen as the cause of the meaning it emits. This is now largely thought to be conferred by various extra-art institutions, grids of knowledge, museums, critics, art worlds, or virtually anything except the behavior of the art object itself. To better understand the intellectual origin of this theoretical tendency I begin with Karl Mannheim and Erwin Panofsky, who argue that knowledge of art's stylistic form does not provide knowledge of its meaning.

In the way that all serious sociological inquiry into the forms of social structure must confront Karl Marx, all serious inquiry into the forms of artistic style structure must confront Heinrich Wolfflin (1950, 1952, 1966), who identified five dimensions on which forms of art systematically vary. Each is discussed as a pair of opposite style tendencies. Two of these seem more primary and probably determine the others. The first pair of opposites is *linear* and *painterly,* referring to the use of line in defining clearly delimited forms versus a less clear line usually attained with a more gestural impressionistic styling. A second pair is *plane* versus *recession,* where plane refers to composition that laterally arranges subjects across the front of the picture, whereas recession refers to subjects and forms receding backward into the picture space.

The other dimensions seem more derivative. *Closed* versus *open* refers to compositions that are either bracketed at the edge or expanding continuously beyond an edge. To some degree such framing is easier with forms that have clear lines defining where they start and stop as opposed to more vague, quivering, and impressionistic (i.e., painterly) edges. It is hard to close the composition when the edge of the form is indeterminate. Then there is *multiplicity* versus *unity. Multiplicity* refers to many separate and equally accented objects within a single composition, whereas *unity* refers to accenting a single object. Again the importance of line and plane. Line allows a clear separation of composite objects, and plane places them next to each other in full view, in contrast to recession, where some may be obscured behind others and hence put in a clearly secondary position. Finally, forms vary in terms of *clearness* versus *unclearness,* which seems very much a consequence of applying linear/painterly and plane/recession principles. Line makes for a clear separation of components in a composition, and plane sets them up to be clearly seen. Painterly practices can make form identification fuzzy or difficult, and utilizing recession can obscure and partially hide, thereby making form seem unclear.

Wolfflin's classic emphasis on the centrality of the formal properties of art generated a counter movement that focused more on art's meaning. In a way somewhat similar to Max Weber's focus on systems of meaning in opposition to Karl Marx's system of class structures, Mannheim and Panofsky sought to identify a necessary independence of art's meaning from Wolfflin's formal arrangement of art's constituent raw materials. In the 1920s, Mannheim (1921–1922) argued for the independent origin of meaning and interpretation, as formal properties of art were like inanimate objects in nature; they could only emit a rather limited objective or factual set of meanings. More generally, he argued that types of meaning go from "objective," the thing in itself without larger implication, to "expressive," what the artist intended, to documentary or "evidential," referring to the outlook of an era. Years later, Panofsky (1955) would make essentially the same argument. In both art history and sociological theory, then, a primacy of form, whether in social relations of production or visual relations of style, was challenged by an assertion of the independent role of ideology and the science of meaning—*verstehen* in Weberian sociology and "iconology" in Panofskyian art analysis. Panofsky argued that art can emit (1) primary, natural, or factual subject matter (pre-iconographic), (2) secondary or conventional subject matter (iconographic), and (3) more intrinsic and general meaning (iconological). The latter are "those underlying principles which reveal the basic attitude of a nation, a period, a class, [or] a religious or philosophical persuasion" (Panofsky 1955:30). These tiers represent a continuum of meaning, ranging from the most literal and specific (primary) to the most general and abstract (iconological), with the iconographic falling in between.

This Mannheim/Panofsky separation of form from meaning reflects a broader tradition of German idealism, where art form, like material object form, is considered objective and factual, a thing that can be studied in and of itself. Natural objects, like paint, bronze, marble, and their structural configuration as a form, cannot by themselves emit larger societal meanings. But art objects do give off such meanings, so they must come from somewhere else, somewhere outside the art object proper. They must, it was reasoned, come from various social understandings, theories, classificatory grids, or art critic interpretations that are read into, or laid upon, art objects. Social significance is now hypothesized to be brought to the object as part of an audience's personal biography, class-based worldview, national temperament, or some other societally generated set of understandings through which the art is perceived and apprehended.

In this way, "every cultural product . . . acquires their separate identity, their neat stratification, within the framework of a theory—i.e., an interpretative theory" (Mannheim 1952:63). Translated: every art form acquires whatever meaning it will have because of its position within a larger theoretical framework. "It may very well be that it is only reflection which introduces this analytic stratified structure in the object which is itself homogenous and non-stratified; and that in the immediately given, pre-theoretical object there is nothing that corresponds to the three strata [of meaning]" (Mannheim 1952:63, 64). Translated: there is nothing about the changing form of art that dictates whether it is capable of only factual/objective interpretation or can symbolically stand for larger, philosophical/religious meanings.

With this assumption the art object became effectively neutered. Art, as a combination of raw materials, is no longer contributing to the meaning it might emit. Meaning is now theorized to come from outside the art object proper. Such a conception unhinges form and interpretation, as signifier (formal compositional structure of art) and signified (meanings, interpretations) become ruptured. What art has to say from this point of view is now read into it by the larger social context. Hence the objects of study in the sociology of art become the art world, critics, gatekeepers, museums, classificatory grids, art theory, and so forth. The sociology and philosophy of art become disciplines where the analysis stops at the easel.

Later philosophers and sociologists of art, from Arthur Danto (1964, 1981) and George Dickie (1974) to Howard Becker (1982) and Pierre Bourdieu (1984, 1993, 1996), all take this position. They differ only in the specific institutional framework that they hypothesize brings meaning to their art object of interest. From this perspective, the art object is now not only interpreted but transformed: "The element under interpretation [the art object] becomes an entirely new unit of meaning when seen under the aspect of formed experience" (Mannheim 1952:68). This assumption is repeated again and again. Consider the following examples illustrative.

> The sociologist is more interested in the social symbolic use of art, rather than the work itself.... All of the re-readings, re-seeings, redefinitions together make up the work of art.... Art is a social construction. (Zolberg 1990:56, 92, 111)
> The work of art ... may disclose significations at different levels according to the deciphering grid applied to it. (Bourdieu 1993:218)
> I suggest that genres represent socially constructed organizing principles that imbue artworks with significance. (DiMaggio 1987:441)
> Becker believes a work of art is what people say it is.... Becker's comments are quite correct. (Alexander 2003:2, 3)
> Sociologists tend now to shift their attention from the meanings and expressive qualities of art and instead focus attention on the ... social conditions of art. (Blau 1989:269)

But can anyone really see anything they want in an art object? In naturally occurring art/audience behavior I think the answer is no, for it is the very shape of art that triggers whether secondary meanings are brought in from the outside. To understand how such change in form affects level of meaning emitted, imagine a hypothetical painting of a bright red barn in a yellow cornfield with a blue sky on a sunny day. When you think about it, you realize there are some requirements necessary to attain the Panofskyan primary meanings of red barn, yellow cornfield, blue sky, and sunny day. The structure of this painting must be a particular combination of pictorial vocabulary, like red, yellow, and blue colors, and particular art-syntactic devices, like rules of perspective for the depth of the barn and shading techniques to create shadows from the sun. Now imagine a second barn painting that is a more abstract rendition: just four plain colorless walls. The form has clearly changed. The structure of the artistic language has been altered. The vocabulary is now reduced. There are no red, yellow, or blue colors, and no constituent forms of barn, corn, sky, or sun. What does this painting now signify? The four seasons, the four corners of the earth, the claustrophobic feeling in a crowded elevator, what? The point is that whereas the realist painting of the objects could say "barn," "corn," "sky," and "sun," this is no longer possible, even if this were somehow the desire of this composition. What has happened is that the shift to a more abstract and minimal code of painterly expression has had direct implications for what can be signified. The range of possible significations is now widened, and with that a greater degree of meaning indeterminacy has arisen. Is this signifier signifying a box, a house, a building, a school, a barn, or just four walls? It simply isn't clear because, semiotically, the painting, by itself, through its own form composition, cannot tell us, for abstract forms create context-dependent artistic communication. That is, abstract signifiers lose their ability to signify any particular signification, and thereby open the door for extra-art interpretation to enter into the meaning-making process. But note: It is only under this very form-specific condition, for meaning shifts are only set in motion by changes in shape or form. The formal properties of art, therefore, are not neutral in the meaning-making process.

Now suppose we create an even more abstract rendition of the barn painting: just four dots. What do these dots signify? The range of possible significations has widened dramatically. They could mean an angry or jovial face, a plant, animal, or human being, or a box, house, building, school, or even a red barn in a yellow cornfield on a sunny day with a blue sky. When the painting is more elaborated (barn, corn, sky, sun), its meaning is constrained; when it becomes more abstract (four walls) the range of meanings widens, and when it becomes even more abstract (four dots) the range of meaning becomes really wide, virtually limitless. This suggests an inverse association between the width of the signifier and the width of possible significations. When a signifier becomes more minimal and abstract, as in the move from barn, corn, sun, and blue sky to four dots, the range of possible significations increases. Signifier (what is actually painted) and signified (what it means) are not, it turns out, separable. Further, increasingly abstract forms become signifiers for ever more generalized and universal ideas rather than specifying realistic, time- and place-bound realities.

The shape of the art object's form triggers higher-level interpretations in the Mannheim/Panofsky sense. They do not arise only from extra-art interpretative grids. But this is not always realized, and the notion that any form can be defined in any way in naturally occurring art/audience behavior persists to the present. Such an emphasis upon non-art object sources of meaning was cemented into place during a period of very abstract and minimal forms, the abstract art of American high modernism after 1945. Whether the art was Abstract Expressionism, Minimalism, or Conceptualism, there arose the idea that the meaning art objects emit derives as much from the theoretical context in which they are interpreted as from their actual look, shape, and form. A consensus soon emerged among critics and aesthetic philosophers. "A contemporary painting or sculpture is a species of centaur—half art materials, half words. The words are the vital energetic element, capable, among other things, of transforming any materials (epoxy, light beams, string, rocks, earth) into art materials" (Rosenberg 1973:151). Pure 1920s Mannheim, rewritten for American abstract art. When Harold Rosenberg argues, "of itself, the eye is incapable of bringing into the intellectual system that today distinguishes between objects that are art and those that are not," he, like Mannheim and Panofsky earlier, omits the point that it is only when certain kinds of forms are semiotically open to multiple significations that they are, of necessity, accompanied by additional theory, interpretation, and iconology to give them their meaning.

The eye only mistakes forms that are so abstract that a specific meaning is not immediately clear. Rosenberg mistakenly blames the naive eye for what is actually a confusion created by restricted form, not ignorant vision:

> Given its primitive function of discriminating among objects in shopping centers and on highways, the eye will recognize a Noland as a fabric design, a Judd as a stack of metal bins—until the eye's outrageous philistinism has been subdued by the drown of formulas concerning breakthroughs in color, space, and even optical perception (this, too, unseen by the eye, of course). It is scarcely an exaggeration to say that paintings are today apprehended with the ears. (Rosenberg 1973:153)

But this blame is misplaced. The eye sees what it sees. To see something that is not there is not the fault of the eye. A Judd sculpture is a stack of bins, just as a Pollock is drips of paint. The problem resides in the form, not the eye. It is the shape of these forms that signify "fabric design" and "stack of bins" rather than "art," for these are context-dependent signifiers requiring more theory or interpretation than their morphology makes possible. But this doesn't hold for less abstract forms. Caravaggio made great use of light, color, and optical perception, but would anyone say this was "unseen by the eye?" Is a Caravaggio apprehended by the ears, by some theory, grid, or iconology, rather than by what is on the canvas? Of course not. The greatness of Raphael, Michelangelo, Rembrandt, Durer, Velázquez, or Titian is not something the eye cannot see.

Whereas a critic during the time of the New York School of abstract art might say, "Frankly, these days, without a theory to go with it, I can't see a painting" (Kramer 1976:4), that certainly would not be said during other, less abstract, periods of art. Such comments are understandable given the pictorial milieu of abstract and minimal art, but it would be a mistake to generalize from a period of highly restricted and minimalist forms to the condition of art in general. This, though, is exactly what happens when philosophers of art such as Danto and Dickie and sociologists such as Bourdieu and Becker argue that what is art depends on what is defined as art by critics, galleries, museums, and dealers who make up the social institutions of the art world. "To see something as art requires something the eye cannot decry—an atmosphere of artistic theory, a knowledge of art: an art world" (Danto 1964:580).

To examine this argument in more detail, consider a hypothetical example provided by Arthur Danto of seven identically painted red squares he claims represent seven different paintings. Painting 1 is the Israelites crossing the Red Sea; Painting 2 is by a Danish portraitist and is called "Kierkegaard's Mood"; Painting 3 is called "Red Square," in Danto's words "a clever bit of Moscow landscape"; Painting 4 is "a minimalist exemplar of geometrical art, which, as it happens, has the same title, 'Red Square'"; Painting 5 is a "metaphysical" work called "Nirvana"; and Painting 6 is called "Red Table Cloth," what he calls "a still-life executed by an embittered disciple of Matisse." There is a number 7, but it is a found object of a red square (Danto 1981:1). Speaking of these seven identical red squares Danto says, "Everything looks the same as everything else, even though the reproductions are of paintings that belong to such diverse genres as historical painting, psychological portraiture, landscape, geometrical abstraction, religious art, and still life" (Danto 1981:2). Notice what he suggests. Whether a painting is a history painting, a portraiture, or a landscape depends solely on defining it as such, with little or no regard for the material reality that exists on the canvas.

Now try another mental experiment. Follow Danto's logic, but with a different painting. Let the form change. Does the Danto theory still apply? Instead of the red square, consider the eighteenth-century Gainsborough portrait of a man and his wife, *Mr. and Mrs. Andrews* (1750). They are painted in front of a big tree, with Mrs. Andrews sitting on a bench and Mr. Andrews standing next to her wearing a three-corner hat. He has a rifle and there is a dog at his feet. They are next to a dirt road with white clouds in a blue sky seen behind them. In naturally occurring art/audience behavior, would this painting be considered Israelites crossing the Red Sea, a Moscow landscape, a red tablecloth, or a piece of geometric art? Probably not, to say the least. The eye would say this is a painting of Mr. and Mrs. Andrews, not a Moscow landscape, not Israelites crossing the Red Sea, and certainly not a red tablecloth.

But why then is it that a red square can be given any number of interpretations, but *Mr. and Mrs. Andrews* cannot? The answer is that the red square is like the four dots discussed earlier. The square's high degree of abstraction yields a restricted signifier, which is formally incapable of signifying any particular signification, hence it is open to being labeled a Moscow landscape, Israelites crossing the Red Sea, or a red tablecloth. The Gainsborough, though, with a much more elaborated form, yields a more constrained interpretation: Mr. and Mrs. Andrews.

Danto, though, doesn't recognize the prerequisite pictorial syntax that makes his model operate. He generalizes about all art. "An object o is then an art work only under an interpretation I, where I is a sort of function that transfigures o into a work: $I(o) = W$. Then even if o is a perceptual constant, variations in I constitute different works" (Danto 1981:125). Now, consider the applicability of this "universal" proposition for both the painting of the red square and the Gainsborough. Different interpretations may transfigure the red square into any number of possible meanings because it has no particular meaning of its own, except the objective, factual, pre-iconographic meaning, "red square." But this isn't true for *Mr. and Mrs. Andrews*, for no iconology, no theory, no interpretation, no art world, can make *Mr. and Mrs. Andrews* into a Moscow landscape or Israelites crossing the Red Sea. The form will not allow itself that interpretation. Therefore an art world cannot transfigure any form it wishes. A collusion of form is necessary. The Institutional Theory of Art, then, only applies to the subset of art objects that are highly abstract and thereby open to having their meaning established by an art world's interpretation. Danto, Dickie, Bourdieu, Becker, and all the other sociologists and philosophers who take this position have mistakenly generalized a specific condition to art in general.

A corrected Danto could be paraphrased as follows: Where there is sufficient elaboration of form, specific meaning is established by form and so the object o is a work of art *without* an interpretation I, which *cannot* transfigure an elaborated realistic form into something it is not. A very abstract form, *af*, since it has no specific meaning in and of itself, is, though, an artwork only under an interpretation I, where I is a semiotic function that transfigures *af* into a work, such that $I(af) = W$. For this limited case of abstract forms the Institutional Theory of Art holds. It is not, though, a general theory of art.

Bringing Wolfflin-like structural properties of art back into theoretical analysis means that art objects are probably more like sentences than like words, that is, more like syntactically structured combinations of elements than word-like single signs. The earlier German idealist assumption that human meaning has to be read into a structural ensemble of art materials has been given a more modern semiotic interpretation with Saussure's (1966) theory of the sign. The separation of form and meaning (Mannheim/Panofsky) can also be represented in semiotic terms when the form is considered a signifier and the meaning its signification. As semiotic theory suggests, there is no necessary relationship between signifier and signification, so there is no relationship between art's formal properties (as a signifier) and its meaning (as a signification).

But an art object has a more complex nature than the Saussurian insight about the relativity of form and meaning in a sign. Art objects are probably closer to sentences—combinations of sign-like constituents to create larger sense-making wholes. It doesn't, for instance, seem unreasonable to consider the combination of dots to make lines, lines to make shapes, and shapes to make a composition such as a painting analogous to the combination of phonemes to make words, words to make phrases, and phrases to make sentences. Because the meaning a sentence emits is not independent of its formal grammatical structure, it is the case that art probably is not independent of its art-syntactic structure.

In discussing the twentieth-century "linguistic turn" in social theory, what is not always noted is that this is largely based on the early Saussure (1966) theory of the relative autonomy of signification from the signifier. This was, though, an insight that worked best for words. There is, for example, no necessary reason why the signifier "dog" has to represent four-legged furry things with tails and cold noses. The signifier "pog" can represent them just as well. But art objects are not as simple. They are more complex structures of many such constituent sign elements. An art object is more a string of such signs, hence more like a sentence. So, yes, "pog" or "dog" is an arbitrary signification for four-legged furry things, but that insight is of less help when we wonder why the form structure, or string of such sign/words, in 1) *Dog bites woman* has a completely different meaning from (2), *Woman bites dog*. That "dog" or "pog" could replace each other says nothing about the overall meaning of the larger composition. To understand that larger complex of meaning that is (1) as opposed to (2), one needs to understand their grammatical structure, or, in our art terms, their style structure. This suggests that some kind of art syntax needs to be identified to fully understand how the complex of constituent elements generates larger sets of meanings in objects such as toys, movies, and sneakers.

These objects might be composed of elements that signify meaning (act like signs), but it is when these individual sign constituents are arranged into a larger composition that we have the art object. And behind the composition's structure are the rules and principles that govern the arrangement of constituent popular culture/art materials (see Bergesen 2000, 2005). For example, the Mixing Model and the Essentially Other Model of Chapter 4 represent preliminary approximations of such an artistic syntax. When followed, they generate objects such as King Kong and Godzilla. Similarly, the permissible combination of body parts, something like an "assembly syntax" for Transformer toys, is what allows them to reincarnate from truck to airplane. A different set of transformational (toy-syntactic) possibilities can only generate differences with a single incarnation, as with GI Joe. The generative syntax of toy-assembly rules dictates whether one toy or the other emits ideas about the philosophy of reincarnation. It is not a "theory of toys," or the cultural "classificatory grid" the child has internalized, that dictates what philosophical principles the toy will emit. To transform from attack vehicle to airplane is an act of reincarnation, no matter what the mindset of the child. And no matter the content of a child's mental classificatory grid, or class-bound attitudes, a toy without such a transforming syntax cannot emit ideas of reincarnation. The same holds for the narrative syntax of what John Rambo can and cannot do that allows him to project quixotic themes. Similarly, the principles of a particular "sneaker-grammar" dictating a balance of color fields and clarity of line in decorative strips makes the Nike Air Jordan I emit a Classic interpretation, whereas rules about the thick crudeness of rubber sole and coarse canvas upper make a Converse Chuck Taylor All-Star sneaker manifest an Archaic style. All of this brings us back to the long-forgotten Heinrich Wolfflin and his syntactic-like discussion of the formal properties of art. His early formulation of the rules of style may eventually make his contribution greater than that of Mannheim or Panofsky.

There is another important and misunderstood aspect to the idea of art forms as grammar that I want to discuss. This is the capacity of social agents to imbue cultural products with social meanings. That is, in terms of the relationship of power and art, syntactically derived flexibility permits social agents to craft specific meanings in accordance with the power and interest of the groups they represent, thereby allowing art to embody social power. This means that the social enters the art process earlier than previously understood, for by the time social interpretations are attached the social message has already been encoded, such that it is simply not the case that "the work of art ... only exists as such for a person who has the means to appropriate it, or in other words, to decipher it" (Bourdieu 1993:220). In fact, we see what we see because of our biological principles of vision, which is where the necessity of our natural being is pressed into service by the historical contingency of our social existence. This allows universal principles of vision to be harnessed by contingent social power. The structuring of art materials by the language of style acts to hierarchically order art elements into a specific art-syntactic structure, such that when light hits this structure and reflects to the eye everyone sees the same thing, regardless of their interpretive grid. That is the constraint of our physical being.

But to say that everyone sees the same art object suggests no room for social variability in meaning, hence no room for crafting social interpretations, hence social meaning must be read into the art object from the outside to attain nuanced interpretation. But what the invariance of vision really means is that when nuanced social messages are encoded within the structure of the art form to begin with, the physical necessity of vision becomes socially harnessed, for social intent is now given inescapable visual necessity. The eye sees what it must see, which means it must also see the art object's grammatical structure, hence the art object's meaning. The underappreciated sociological point is that the shape of the form is the grammatical structure through which human agency is made mandatory viewing because of the harnessed principles of vision.

Sight isn't neutral and is given its social quality through the structured placement of art materials, which occurs before interpretive grids are laid upon them. That is, it isn't so much the interpretive grid of, say, a class-bound way of looking at the world but the shape of the art itself that affects not only what is seen, but what is understood. Therefore, the ability to make "distinctions" (Bourdieu 1984) is not so much a product of the unequal distribution of ideas about aesthetics, but of differences in the form of the art that is seen. That the Baroque looks different from the Neoclassical isn't a matter of different interpretive grids saying "Baroque" versus "Neoclassical" that have been laid upon, say, a square of red paint. Instead it is different movements of paint, line, color, and shading—that is, different grammatical form structures of art. Most important, because these structured movements of art materials constitute the meaning-constraining syntax of art, this is where art's meaning arises. The eye is actually coerced into making "distinctions" by the form upon which it gazes; it has no choice, and this is what gives cultural objects their power.

If social power were merely a matter of classificatory grids, interpretations, expert opinion, and so forth, individuals could agree or disagree. Social power, though, enters prior to sight, in the very construction of the cultural object. Once the work is made, the majority of its meaning-emitting potential is set in place. All the talk of art worlds, classificatory grids, habituses, and so forth, is largely secondary.

Structured art materials, then, give popular culture and art their social quality, for through the form they take, sight is coerced. Which means, contrary to the twentieth-century idealist turn in social theory, sight, determined by form, precedes interpretive frame; and not only that, but sight, preceding interpretive grid, is the most fundamental source of the social in art. Art forms do not need external interpretation to yield social meaning, for the power of culture lies in its forms, not in the secondary act of interpretive framing. Recent efforts at moving explanation to extra-art interpretive frames have only obfuscated the way in which power manifests itself as art. It has been one of the purposes of this book to correct this error by bringing the cultural object back into sociological analysis.

References

Alexander, Victoria D. 2003. *Sociology of the Arts: Exploring Fine and Popular Forms*. Malden, MA: Blackwell.

Arrighi, Giovanni. 2005a. "Hegemony Unravelling—1." *New Left Review* 32: 23–80.

———. 2005b. "Hegemony Unravelling—2." *New Left Review* 33: 83–116.

Auerbach, Erich. 1969. "Enchanted Dulcinea," in Lowry Nelson, ed., *Cervantes: A Collection of Critical Essays*, 98–122. Englewood Cliffs, NJ: Prentice Hall.

Becker, Howard S. 1982. *Art Worlds*. Berkeley: University of California Press.

Berger, Peter. 1969. *The Sacred Canopy*. Garden City, NJ: Anchor.

Berger, Peter, and Thomas Luckmann. 1966. *The Social Construction of Reality*. Garden City, NJ: Doubleday.

Bergesen, Albert J. 1984. *The Sacred and the Subversive: Political Witch-Hunts as National Rituals*. Storrs, CT: Society for the Scientific Study of Religion Monograph Series.

———. 1996. "The Art of Hegemony," in Sing C. Chew and Robert Denemark, eds., *The Underdevelopment of Development: Essays in Honor of Andre Gunder Frank*, 259–278. Thousand Oaks, CA: Sage.

———. 2000. "A Linguistic Model of Art History." *Poetics* 28: 73–90.

———. 2005. "Culture and Cognition," in Mark Jacobs and Nancy Hanrahan (eds.) *The Blackwell Companion to the Sociology of Culture*. New York: Basil Blackwell.

Bergesen, Albert J., and John Sonnett. 2001. "The Global 500: Mapping the World Economy at Century's End." *American Behavioral Scientist* 44: 1602–1615.

Bielby, William T., and Denise D. Bielby. 1999. "Organizational Mediation of Project-Based Labor Markets: Talent Agencies and the Careers of Screenwriters." *American Sociological Review* 64: 64–85.

Blau, Judith. 1989. *The Shape of Culture: A Study of Contemporary Cultural Patterns in the United States*. New York: Cambridge University Press.

Blumer, H. 1969. *Symbolic Interaction*. Berkeley: University of California Press.

Bourdieu, Pierre. 1984. *Distinction: A Social Critique of the Judgment of Taste.* Cambridge, MA: Harvard University Press.

———. 1993. *The Field of Cultural Production.* New York: Columbia University Press.

———. 1996. *The Rules of Art: Genesis and Structure of the Literary Field.* Stanford, CA: Stanford University Press.

Canby, Vincent. 1985. "Movie Review." *New York Times,* May 22, C23.

Cervantes, Miguel de. 1981. *Don Quixote.* Trans. John Ormsby, ed. Joseph R. Jones and Kenneth Douglas. New York: W. W. Norton.

Chase-Dunn, Christopher. 1998. *Global Formation: Structures of the World-Economy.* Lanham, MD: Rowman and Littlefield.

Danto, Arthur. 1964. "The Artworld." *Journal of Philosophy* 61: 571–584.

———. 1981. *The Transfiguration of the Commonplace.* Cambridge, MA: Harvard University Press.

Dehio, Ludwig. 1962. *The Precarious Balance.* New York: Vintage.

DeNora, Tia. 1991. "Musical Patronage and Social Change in Beethoven's Vienna." *American Journal of Sociology* 97: 310–346.

De Riquer, Martin. 1981. "Cervantes and the Romances of Chivalry," in *Don Quixote,* ed. Joseph R. Jones and Kenneth Douglas, 895–913. New York: W. W. Norton.

Dickie, George. 1974. *Art and the Aesthetic: An Institutional Analysis.* Ithaca, NY: Cornell University Press.

DiMaggio, Paul. 1977. "Market Structure, the Creative Process, and Popular Culture: Toward an Organizational Reinterpretation of Mass-Culture Theory." *Journal of Popular Culture* 3: 436–452.

———. 1987. "Classification in Art." *American Sociological Review* 52: 440–455.

Douglas, Mary. 1966. *Purity and Danger.* Harmondsworth, UK: Penguin.

———. 1970. *Natural Symbols.* New York: Pantheon.

Durkeim, Emile. 1933. *The Division of Labor in Society.* Glencoe, IL: Free Press.

———. 1965 [1912]. *The Elementary Forms of the Religious Life.* Glencoe, IL: Free Press.

Durkheim, Emile, and Marcel Mauss. 1963. *Primitive Classification.* Chicago: University of Chicago Press.

Fine, Gary Alan. 1992. "The Culture of Production: Aesthetic Choices and Constraints in Culinary Work." *American Journal of Sociology* 97: 1268–1294.

Giddens, Anthony. 1990. *The Consequences of Modernity.* Stanford: Stanford University Press.

Goffman, Erving. 1959. *The Presentation of Self in Everyday Life.* Garden City, NJ: Doubleday.

Halberstam, David. 1999. *Playing for Keeps: Michael Jordan and the World He Made.* New York: Random House.

Haraway, Donna. 1991. *Simians, Cyborgs and Women: The Reinvention of Nature.* London: Free Association.

Hauser, Arnold. 1959. *The History of Art.* Vol. 2. New York: Vintage Press.

———. 1965. *Mannerism: The Crisis of the Renaissance and the Origin of Modern Art.* Cambridge, MA: Harvard University Press.

Ichiro, Hori, Ikado Fujio, Wakimoto Tsuneya, and Yanagawa Keichi, eds. 1981. *Japanese Religion: A Survey by the Agency for Cultural Affairs.* Tokyo: Kodansha International.

Kaufman, Jason. 2004. "Endogenous Explanation in the Sociology of Culture." *Annual Review of Sociology* 30: 335–357.

Kennedy, Paul. 1987. *The Rise and Fall of the Great Powers.* New York: Vintage.

Kiefer, Kit. 2000. "Fly Me to the Moon: A Sailor Moon TV-Episode Guide." *Pojo's Collector Card World* 1, 2 (June/July): 88–95.

Kindleberger, Charles P. 1996. *World Economic Primacy, 1500–1990.* New York: Oxford.

Kopkind, Andrew. 1985. "Movie Review," *Nation* 240 (June 22): 776–777.

Kramer, Hilton. 1976. Quoted in Tom Wolfe, *The Painted Word.* New York: Bantam.

LaFeber, Walter. 2002. *Michael Jordan and the New Global Capitalism.* New York: W. W. Norton.

Lees, J. D., and M. Cerasini. 1998. *The Official Godzilla Compendium.* New York: Random House.

Leys, Simon. 1998. "The Imitation of Our Lord Don Quixote." *New York Review of Books* 45: 32–35.

Lieberson, Stanley. 2003. *A Matter of Taste: How Names, Fashions, and Culture Change.* New Haven, CT: Yale University Press.

Mancing, Howard. 1982. *The Chivalric World of Don Quijote: Style, Structure, and Narrative Technique.* Columbia: University of Missouri Press.

Mannheim, Karl. 1921–1922. "On the Interpretation of *Weltanschauung.*" *Jahrbuch fur Kunstgeschichte* 1, 15.

———. 1952. "On the Interpretation of *Weltanschauung,*" in K. Mannheim, *Essays in the Sociology of Knowledge,* 33–83. New York: Oxford University Press.

Mead, George Herbert. 1934. *Mind, Self, and Society.* Chicago: University of Chicago Press.

Mills, C. Wright. 1940. "Situated Actions and Vocabularies of Motive." *American Sociological Review* 5 (December): 904–913.

Morgan, H. T. 1942. *Chinese Symbols and Superstitions.* South Pasadena, CA: P. D. and Ione Perkins.

Nelson, Benjamin. 1981. *On the Roads to Modernity: Conscience, Science, and Civilizations—Selected Writings.* Lanham, MD: Rowman and Littlefield.

Onishi, Norimitsu. 2005. "Why Japan Seems Content to Be Run by One Party." *New York Times,* September 7, A4.

Panofsky, Erwin. 1955. *Meaning in the Visual Arts*. Chicago: University of Chicago Press.

Peterson, Richard A., and N. Anand. 2004. "The Production of Culture Perspective." *Annual Review of Sociology*, vol. 30, (August): 311–334.

Pierce, John J. 1998. "Godzilla beyond the Atomic Age: A Monster for All Seasons," in J. D. Lees and Marc Cerasini, *The Official Godzilla Compendium*, 17. New York: Random House.

Rasler, Karen A., and William R. Thompson. 1994. *The Great Powers and Global Struggle, 1490–1990*. Lexington: University of Kentucky Press.

Resnick, Rick. 1988. "Plastics Help Give Hightops Their High Tops." *Sports Illustrated*, March 30: 44.

Rosenberg, Harold. 1973. "Art and Words," in *Idea Art*, ed. Gregory Battcock, 150–164. New York: E. P. Dutton.

Saussure, Ferdinand de. 1966. *Course in General Linguistics*. New York: McGraw-Hill.

Sewell, William Jr. 1992. "A Theory of Structure: Duality, Agency, and Transformation." *American Journal of Sociology* 98: 1–29.

Strasser, J. B., and Laurie Becklund. 1993. *Swoosh: The Unauthorized Story of Nike and the Men Who Played There*. New York: Harper Business.

Swidler, Ann. "Culture in Action: Symbols and Strategies." *American Sociological Review* 51: 273–286.

Vasari, G. 1977. *The Lives of the Painters, Sculptors, and Architects*. 4 vols. Trans. G. du C. DeVere. New York: Henry N. Abrams.

Wallerstein, Immanuel. 1974. *The Modern World-System: Capitalist Agriculture and the Origins of the European World-Economics in the Sixteenth Century*. New York: Academic Press.

Warner, William. 1992. "Spectacular Action: Rambo and the Popular Pleasures of Pain," in Lawrence Grossberg, Cary Nelson, and Paula Teichler, eds., *Cultural Studies*, 672–688. New York: Routledge.

Watt, Ian. 1996. *Myths of Modern Individualism: Faust, Don Quixote, Don Juan, Robinson Crusoe*. Cambridge: Cambridge University Press.

Wolfflin, Heinrich. 1950 [1915]. *Principles of Art History: The Problem of the Development of Style in Later Art*. Trans. M. D. Hottinger. New York: Dover Publications.

———. 1952 [1898]. *Classic Art: The Great Masters of the Italian Renaissance*. London: Phaidon Press.

———. 1966 [1888]. *Renaissance and Baroque*. Ithaca, NY: Cornell University Press.

Wuthnow, Robert. 1987. *Meaning and Moral Order: Explorations in Cultural Analysis*. Berkeley: University of California Press.

Zolberg, Vera. 1990. *Constructing a Sociology of the Arts*. New York: Cambridge University Press.

Index

Abstract Expressionism, 110
Accent lines, 34, 36
Achelous, 69
Adidas, 15; development of, 12; logo of, 12, 16; Pro Model of, 12, 15, 17 (photo)
Air Jordan, 15, 25; balance/proportion of, 19–20; Classic effect of, 36; photo of, 24, 32; weight of, 21
Air Jordan I, 11, 115; heel of, 40n4; photo of, 18; success for, 16
Air Jordan XIV, 40n5
Air Max Plus, 40n6
Air Penny, 40n5
Air Terra Goatek, 40n6
"Air Zoom GP" shoe, 25, 27
Alien (movie), 66
All of Me (movie), 71
Amsterdam Olympics (1928), 11
Anaconda (movie), 66
Anubis, 69
Archaic, 10, 115
Archaic sneakers, 11, 13, 15, 16, 19, 25, 39; decline of, 20
Art: formal compositional structure of, 108, 109; general theory of, 113; Greek, 38, 39; meaning of, 8, 117; philosophy of, 108; popular culture and, 2, 7; power

and, 115; as social construction, 108; sociology of, 7, 8, 108
Art historical styles, 5–6, 9, 10
Art objects, 8, 9, 107, 114, 115; behavior of, 105; grammatical structure of, 116; neutering of, 108; observing, 109; social variability and, 116
Athens Olympics (1896), 11
Attack of the 50-Foot Woman, The (movie), 66
Autobots, 78

Barkley, Charles, 23
Barkley shoes, 39n3; Mannerist effect of, 36
Baroque, 1, 2, 5, 9, 10; High Renaissance and, 21; movement and, 27; neoclassical and, 116; shift to, 33
Baroque sneakers, 1, 11, 21, 23, 25, 27, 30, 33; asymmetrical effect of, 30, 32 (photo); color of, 34; photo of, 26, 29, 31; self and, 36; solemnity of, 37; sole of, 27, 28 (photo); transition to, 39
Base-Superstructure Model, 3, 4
Batman, 63, 87, 89, 90
Battle of Lepanto, 60n2

126 ✳ Index

About the Author

Albert J. Bergesen is Professor of Sociology at the University of Arizona. He is the author of numerous books and articles. He coauthored *God in the Movies* (2003) with Andrew M. Greeley and *Cultural Analysis: The Work of Peter Berger, Mary Douglas, Michel Foucault, and Jürgen Habermas* (1984) with Wuthnow, Hunter, and Kurtzweil.